MARCH F

March for Jesus

**GRAHAM KENDRICK, GERALD COATES,
ROGER FORSTER AND LYNN GREEN
WITH
CATHERINE BUTCHER**

**KINGSWAY PUBLICATIONS
EASTBOURNE**

ISBN 0 86065 987 9

Printed in Great Britain for
KINGSWAY PUBLICATIONS LTD
Lottbridge Drove, Eastbourne, E Sussex BN 23 6NT by
Clays Ltd, St. Ives plc.
Typeset by J&L Composition Ltd, Filey, North Yorkshire

Contents

	Preface	7
1.	Four Friends	9
2.	The City March	27
3.	The Westminster March	41
4.	The Torch March	56
5.	March for Jesus Across the Nation	70
6.	Out of the Flames	82
7.	A Response to the Critics	88
8.	March for Jesus Where You Live	97
9.	Prayer March Across the Nation	108
10.	Dynamic Growth	116
11.	Going Global	126
	Appendix: March for Jesus Theology	134

Preface

Marching isn't new. The children of Israel marched out of
Egypt, round the walls of Jericho, and into the Promised
Land. The annual marches to Jerusalem for the great
festivals of Passover, Tabernacles and Pentecost became
part of the pattern of life in which Jesus participated. He
too led festive followers into Jerusalem as part of the
Passover march on what we now know as Palm Sunday.

In more modern times Wesley tentatively led worshippers
out into the open air, but was ostracised for it; the Salvation
Army march even though, last century, some were stoned
for it; and Anglicans still march to beat the bounds of
parishes and remember the Great Commission on Rogation
Sunday, though this rural practice receives little publicity.

Faith and marching have often gone together but have
not always found favour with the establishment. March for
Jesus is much the same: many take part gladly; some come
along out of curiosity; others criticise it openly.

March for Jesus did not start in a committee room with
church leaders trying to find a new way to mobilise the
church. It started spontaneously as four friends were
prompted to lead believers out onto the streets. The four
were not part of the traditional denominations, yet many
people from every section of the Christian community, in
different countries around the world, have responded with
enthusiasm.

March for Jesus emerged in the UK out of earnest prayer.

7

The Ichthus Christian Fellowship, Youth With A Mission (UK) and the Pioneer Trust were mobilised by the fact that evangelism was not bearing fruit in England to the same extent as in other parts of the globe. Meanwhile worship pioneer Graham Kendrick was at the forefront of a movement that simply brought worshippers out of their church buildings, whatever the consequences may be, evangelistic or otherwise. As they prayed and responded to what they felt God was asking them to do, they found that their evangelism began to bear fruit. When they asked: 'Why? What elements combined to make this more effective?' they discovered that marching and praying were two of the common factors. And when the leaders of these groups realised that they were finding the same answer, the movement now known as March for Jesus was born.

It began as the leaders of these three groups and Graham Kendrick brought their ministries together in response to what God seemed to be doing. As the years have gone on their co-operation has developed as a simple principle is put into practice: they listen to God, watch what is happening in the world and devote their energies to what God seems to be blessing.

March for Jesus has never had, nor has now, a hidden agenda which stretches far into the future. The four: Roger Forster, Gerald Coates, Lynn Green and Graham Kendrick want to see God's kingdom come in Britain and to the ends of the earth. Together with others they have sought God and have been open to listen to his directions. They see themselves as the custodians of a vision which God is revealing. God writes the agenda. They seek to respond, continually giving away that vision and watching to see what God does next.

This book tells the story of how four different men and their ministries came together; it describes their hopes, dreams and visions, and it explains what has happened as they have sought to obey God wholeheartedly. But this is not a history book. In showing why so many believers now march for Jesus, it gives a reason and a proved method for those who want to play their part in fulfilling the Great Commission Jesus gave to 'go into all the earth. . .'.

I

Four Friends

Over the past twenty years Gerald Coates has been at the heart of what has been dubbed the 'house church movement' in Britain. As well as being the founder of Pioneer Trust, and leader of the Pioneer Team caring for and planting churches, he oversees almost 100 fellowships. Together with Dr Patrick Dixon, he was a founding member of the AIDS initiative ACET, which is now caring for more dying AIDS patients in their homes than any other charity.

Gerald sees March for Jesus as 'a radical statement that God is at work in our nation'. How did it begin for him? Gerald explains:

'In the late sixties and early seventies I would often ask in prayer, 'How do you reach a nation?' In September 1971 I stood beside Lord Longford in Trafalgar Square with 30,000 people as part of the Nationwide Festival of Light. They marched to Hyde Park where another group of several thousand was waiting for them. I never thought I would see such crowds again—but I was wrong.

The best things are usually stumbled upon accidentally. We look back and realise that God must have been in them. It is not plans, personalities or numbers which bring glory to God, but things performed by the Spirit. God himself has been at work in March for Jesus in a special way, without us realising it!

Roger Forster, Lynn Green, Graham Kendrick and I have been friends for years. We met on several occasions to pray about taking the praise and prayers of the charismatic movement out onto the streets. But we didn't have a grand strategy. Almost everything that God does is pushed from the ground up rather than imposed from above down. We tapped into a grassroots movement which we weren't even sure was there; a grassroots movement which is hungry for spiritual life, hungry for Scripture, wanting to be useful.

This movement can be seen throughout Britain as evangelical churches of every type have been growing. It has been slow, but it's becoming increasingly rapid. Yet most of this growth has taken place in buildings. Within these buildings there has been growing love, trust and respect. Division and suspicion among church leaders has been giving way to relational unity and friendship.

We have responded to the desire of evangelicals to be seen to be together, praying and loving and blessing each other; growing in faith together, encouraging each other, not allowing the enemy to divide; saying that, for all our differences doctrinally and methodologically, we love each other and want to believe in each other and speak well of each other.

That's what heaven is like. God the Father, God the Son and God the Holy Spirit are in relationship. They are friends; they believe in each other. They want each other to succeed. We have sought to reflect that in our relationships with each other.

Roger, Graham, Lynn and myself are grateful to God for the friendship he has given us. We have nurtured it and God has given us something to do with that friendship. Apart from eating and drinking together—remembering that table fellowship was important to Jesus' ministry—we have found ourselves on the same platforms, and have learned from each other as we have contributed to various joint initiatives.

We have grown to trust each other. If trust was to break down, progress would be impossible. Lack of trust is why so many local and national initiatives either take so long to strategise or simply never materialise. The lack of trust and the long time deep trust takes to build, leaves room for others to get on and plan their own evangelistic, church planting, prayer or youth events without reference to anybody else. That is not how we have operated.

But we have not sought to establish a carefully blended mix of leaders with a balance of representatives from each group. We have followed a movement of God's Spirit and the key is in the relationships: in worship, in caring, in faith, in praise—all the stuff that's in heaven; people loving one another, blessing one another, worshipping the Lord, caring for each other; with no gossip and no character assassination.

Doctrinal unity is important in terms of the foundations of our faith, but it seems everyone who comes together on doctrinal unity ends up splitting. Church history is littered with excellent churches who came together as a result of God's Spirit moving, but ended up defining doctrine and becoming a spent force. Now they are irrelevant and ineffective.

Then there are those who strive for methodological unity—this nit-picking fundamentalist evangelical approach to Scripture that asks questions like, 'Where is marching in the Bible?' They never had that approach in the New Testament. When Peter walked down the streets and his shadow fell on someone and they got healed, we don't hear his disciples say, 'Could you please not get healed because we haven't got a Bible verse for it. This has never been done before.' It's an absurd way of treating the Scriptures. Where healing is concerned, if in the end nothing has happened, then we have to question methods; methods are important, but we are not primarily looking for methodological unity. We are primarily looking for relational unity.

It is surprising to think that when God had made the world and his masterpiece, man, there was still something that he said was 'not good'. Genesis tells us it wasn't good that Adam was on his own. He was made for relationships. This creation principle is at the heart of all we four have sought to do.

Sharing the same platforms has also contributed to our unity. I cannot think of another country with a finer network of relationships, especially among evangelical leaders. Initiatives like Spring Harvest, others launched by the Evangelical Alliance, and the wide range of private forums have furthered trust and unity. But our unity is not to create a power base to make us feel better or bigger! Jesus' prayer for unity in John 17 is 'that the world may know'.

We have wanted to give the church a new visible face. It's a dangerous remedy for those who prefer things to stay the same—but a wonderful remedy for those who believe Christ's body must be seen to be effective. We want to bring Christianity out of buildings on to the streets; to give Christians a chance to be seen together rather than apart; to give a display of love, unity and joy, offering a real opportunity to Christians to say sorry to believers of other persuasions for superior attitudes and competitive spirits.

We haven't tried to 'make something happen' for the Decade of Evangelism. We have followed the Holy Spirit and have responded to the rising tide of believers who want to be visible, lovable and available. Rather than haranguing the public with the Good News in a confrontational style— which they read as Bad News—we have looked for ways to get out there and take a little bit of heaven with us.

If anyone asked, 'Have you always wanted to be a voice to the nation?' I'd say, 'Yes, of course.' I've always wanted to see the whole land spread with the gospel. Of course I want people in the House of Commons and the royal family to hear the name of Jesus, and every other person in the land. But we didn't set out a specific strategy to reach these people or try to follow a single theological principle. We have followed the Spirit to see what he is doing.

The way we do our theology in the UK and the Western world has until recently had very little to do with life. In the New Testament they only discovered their theology after it had happened. Nobody really believed a virgin would conceive; nobody really believed that the Creator of the cosmos would be hung upon a cross and every bone would be disjointed. It was all there in the Scriptures, but nobody really believed any of these things until they happened. Then suddenly revelation came: 'You are the Christ—the Son of the living God.' Peter suddenly saw it. But he saw it only after the event.

It has been the same with March for Jesus. Nobody believed British Christians would take to the streets in their thousands. Nobody believed Christians from different streams and denominations would march together across the nation. Nobody believed that it would be possible to take the walls off the church in every European capital—East and West. But with hindsight, we can see God has been leading us.

Psalm 133 says that wherever God's people dwell together in unity God commands a blessing. God commands his blessing on anything that bears the stamp of heaven. If our lives and the way we relate to each other have these marks of heaven, God commands his blessing on us. There's quite a difference living under the commanded blessing of God and desperately trying to get blessed. We have sought to live in that blessing, responding to God's Spirit, presenting the visible, lovable and available church to the world.'

Lynn Green, British-based Director of Youth With A Mission for Europe, the Middle East and Africa, takes up the March for Jesus phenomenon from his perspective:
'The roots of Youth With A Mission's involvement with March for Jesus go back to 1980, when God did something in my life regarding faith for London.

I moved from the United States to England in 1970, but I never rose above London's spiritually depressing atmosphere. I arrived in winter and my earliest impressions were of long, cold, grey days in an inadequately heated flat. I travelled by train into central London on business, and could see the backs of all these houses each representing four to six people, hundreds of thousands of them—all with those little chimneys—stretching to the horizon, and I had no faith that God could work in the city.

During my first ten years in Britain we moved our YWAM

training base into Sussex and began to establish a national work. But in 1980 God dropped faith into my heart. I began to see that he was going to change the scene, and with that came a commitment to prayer. For me, that's when March for Jesus began.

I started praying for London and rallying YWAM to pray for London. By 1981 nine guys were meeting every Tuesday night and our wives would join us on alternate weeks. We met from 8pm until at least midnight, sometimes until 2am, for an open-ended evening of serious prayer. In YWAM our prayers are always into evangelism, always for getting people saved. We focused more on central London and were asking, 'Lord, why aren't we making progress?' We weren't getting any housing for the new team members, and we weren't finding any premises in London for outreach centres.

We found several redundant properties, but the Christian organisations who owned them were not prepared to lease, let, or sell at less than the market price; so developers bought them. It was very frustrating to say 'There's an ideal house' or 'There's an ideal shop-front for an outreach centre', only to find there was no question of anybody doing anything other than get top market money for it. We even saw one fantastic place come on the market and sell for market value, and all the while the trustees had no idea what they would do with the money. They were driven to get the top price for it, and when they did get the money they tried to work out what to do with it and, in the end, it was squandered.

These dead-ends led us to say, 'God what is going on? Why are we making no progress?' It was then that we felt that God spoke to us about greed and unrighteous trade.

It happened when my wife Marti and I, together with our associate directors Barry and Kay Austin, met for prayer for London. We were going to be the core of the team that went to live in London. At the end of the summer of 1982, we had worked in Earls Court and had seen a number of people come to the Lord, but we still had no beach-head for a team to move in and carry on. So we were asking God why. When we came to prayer, Kay said, 'This morning I

felt God spoke to me out of the passage about the spies
going into the land of Canaan —when they were discovering
what their enemy was like.' She said, 'I believe the Lord is
saying that, if we ask, he wants to tell us something of the
nature of the battle that we're in.'

That seemed right. It was a little bit of a new idea to
us then, but we prayed and God prompted us—each
independently—about this theme of greed and unrighteous
trade. I had a passage of Scripture along with it that
gradually made more and more sense. It has become one
of the primary foundation stones in my understanding of
spiritual warfare.

Ezekiel 27 is the passage that was brought alive to me.
In the New International Version the heading is 'A lament
for Tyre'. And after the lament for Tyre, the first ten verses
of Ezekiel 28 are addressed to 'The ruler of Tyre,' and here
it is quite clear who he is talking to. It is a lament or an
oracle against the man who was king, the ruler of Tyre.
'You are a man not a god . . . You think you are god . . .'
But then it changes at verse 11 and the next nine verses are
against the King of Tyre. Here it says 'You were the model
of perfection . . . you were in Eden, the garden of God . . .
on the day you were created they were prepared . . . you
were blameless in your ways until wickedness was found in
you. Through your widespread trade, you were filled with
violence . . .'

Tyre was the capital of the Phoenicians. It was the
wealthiest centre of the time, the trading centre, and it was
almost as if this demonic being, who considered himself
equal with God, Lucifer, the devil, was yoked together with
the King of Tyre, the man. He was the power behind the
throne.

We were praying for London which has been the trading
centre of the world for 800 years, so we recognised the
similarities. It wasn't because we were developing any new
prayer theories, we were just trying to pray for a breakthrough in London and this strategy really made sense to us.

However, I'm always cautious about subjective guidance.

There were four of us and we were independently getting
similar things from God, but we were all in the same room
and I wanted more confirmation than that. Over the next
two months I had two different people come to me. One of
them was Stuart McAlpine who pastors a church in
Washington DC, and has been a long-time friend. He visited
Britain about two months after we got that word, in the
autumn of 1982, and he said, 'I've been praying for London
and I feel God's spoken to me.' He felt God was saying a
principality or spiritual force of evil—like those described
in Ephesians 6:12—was at work over the capital. Stuart
called it 'greed and unrighteous exchange'.

About that time, we learned that Jesus sends us out as
sheep in the midst of wolves, in the opposite spirit to the
spirit in the world or the enemy. Therefore, I thought that
it was wise to find out the nature of what we were against,
and then to look out for testing in that area. As we thought
that our enemy's nature was greed and unrighteous trade
we began being more generous and to be sure that we were
completely honest in all dealings. We increased our giving,
all of us—individually and YWAM as a whole.

Within a year of starting to pray about London in this
way, Toc H, a Christian organisation, released a hostel for
us to use temporarily. Fifty of us moved into London.
Throughout that time we were having periodic prayer
meetings and sometimes Graham Kendrick joined us. The
meetings varied. We had half nights of prayer and days of
prayer. We called all the YWAM people in England together
at St Mark's, Kennington, and we had days of prayer and
fasting.

We were having a miserable time with our work in Earls
Court. We could hardly step on the street without getting
arrested for obstruction. The police did not want us doing
open-air meetings; they did not want us doing street
evangelism; they did not want us visiting from pub to pub.
There was antipathy and we weren't getting anywhere. On
one occasion we were standing to the south of Earls Court
Station, trying to hold an open-air meeting, and a guy two

floors up opened his window and threw a bucket of water over us. With this kind of open antagonism we abandoned our outreach until we thought we'd made a breakthrough in prayer.

We devoted time to prayer and within a day we felt God saying 'march'. About 125 of us marched up Earls Court Road and down Warwick Road carrying banners, singing, praising and worshipping as we went. We marched two or three days in a row, and when we finished the atmosphere was different. Since then we've had a permanent presence at Earls Court and many people have become Christians there, including people out of the homosexual movement.

We felt that we were onto something after this breakthrough. It was a prayer strategy that we'd never seen before and we were excited by it. In 1985 we had a day of prayer for London, and then came the feeling that we had to go out on the streets in a similar way. By now we were beginning to think that the principalities, powers and spiritual strongholds had historical roots, so we looked into different parts of the City of London where we felt there was a stronghold of greed and unrighteous trade. We prayed in the morning at St Mark's, then went out and prayed at different locations, especially the old locations of London's City Gates. It was such a good day that we planned to do it again and let a few friends know.

Graham Kendrick joined us for a similar day in 1986 when we met at the City Temple in Holborn. After a time of praise and prayer we divided into groups and walked to significant City locations where we prayed before joining together again at the Royal Exchange for a final declaration of the lordship of Christ.

Originally London grew because of its location on a river suitable for trade and commerce. It was a busy trade city from Roman times. Before that, when there was a Celtic civilisation, it appears that the gods of commerce and trade were worshipped there. One of the sources of the name of London could have been the Celtic god Lug, who was worshipped as the god of light and the god of trade and commerce in the area which we know as London. (Peter Adams, a colleague within YWAM, has done much research in this area.)

I think there is a direct link between greed and the most pressing problems in London today—whether it is housing, unemployment or drug addiction. And our days of spiritual warfare were held in London to help make a break from the past. We wanted a different spiritual atmosphere in Britain's capital city.

That's what those days of spiritual warfare were about. Even a few people interceding on behalf of others can be effective. God is just but he is also merciful. Those days of prayer encouraged us to be available to God, to 'stand in the gap' and pray for mercy towards ourselves and others who don't deserve it.

As we ended the day in 1986 at the Royal Exchange we prayed: 'Use this day to stir up your people across the land. Stir us up, Lord; stir us up across the nation. You have a mighty army, wake us up that we might arise and march forward, organised, understanding, listening to you, following your tactics, battling in obedience to you, our commander.'

When we heard Ichthus were planning a London event and prayer and praise were to be part of it, we wanted to be involved. I had a long-standing friendship with Roger Forster and Gerald Coates. Graham had already been involved in our days of prayer, so we joined forces and said, 'We ought to do this together'.'

Roger Forster, leader of the 3,000–member Ichthus Fellowship in South East London, explains how he began marching for Jesus:
'Being out in the street is not a new part of my personal ministry. In more than thirty years as an evangelist I've always done a fair amount of street work. In fact I virtually began my ministry standing on street corners giving out tracts.

When the Ichthus Christian Fellowship began in 1974, it

was our regular practice to be in the shopping areas, along the streets. There was always this aspect of going out into the open to stand up and be counted for Christ.

It was in those early days that I began to notice that a change took place when we were more public and visible. I was aware that something was happening in the heavens as we were doing things on earth. The awareness was subjective, but others also sensed that we were affecting the spiritual condition of the area simply by being out in the open and witnessing before heaven and earth.

In Ichthus we often march through neighbourhoods before planting a congregation. We prayerwalk up and down the streets, have praise marches through the area, and finally establish a new congregation in a public building. We now have forty congregations in different places throughout South East London and three on the north side of the river. Most were planted after a similar process of prayerwalking and public praise.

As a fellowship we have always been in mission. Sometimes we take part in local carnivals, fitting in and doing our bit. Sometimes we arrange our own carnival-type marches before, during or after missions. Sometimes we put a tent up, other times we take a hall, but we are always doing something in an effort to evangelise. Praise marches in themselves act as a witness. People come and talk to us and join us as we go along.

In one area we did some prayer and praise marches through a local housing estate. When they held their own festival, they insisted that our Ichthus band lead the event. The local authority was backing the festival, so they had to publicise the fact that it was an Ichthus band taking the lead. They also had to announce our evangelistic meeting which was being held during the festival on the housing estate. Ironically, it was the same local authority that, a few months before, had refused to sell us surplus school equipment because we had opposed them on the issue of promoting homosexuality through local council structures.

In another area we held an open-air meeting in one

neighbourhood after a race riot. Shops had been looted and many were boarded up. People were glowering at each other across the street when we marched into the shopping area. As we stood there, worshipping and praising God, the atmosphere changed; people smiled and laughed again, black and white began to talk together.

On another occasion, in a different area, we were told that the power connected with a local coven of witches had been restricted because we were holding an open-air event in a nearby high street. We should not be surprised by this, and I'm glad to say there have been many such examples in our experience.

March for Jesus began for us as we started to work in Soho, London's red light district. John Pressdee, one of the Ichthus ministry team, had asked God to give him a prayer burden for London. Opportunities to work in theatre-land opened up: Laurence Singlehurst of Youth With A Mission offered the use of premises in Leicester Square and we began to plant a church there. That was towards the end of 1985 and, as part of the church planting process, we arranged a march around Soho.

It was a Friday night, in early 1986, and we only expected a few people to turn up. But 300 people came to Leicester Square! We set off, walking in pairs and singing our way round Soho, and had an extraordinary reception from the prostitutes—they all came out, cheered, and asked us to sing for them.

We sang round Soho, stopping to pray for specific places. Then we went back into the basement of Orange Street Congregational Church and worshipped God as we dedicated the Leicester Square premises to the Lord.

Not more than a few weeks later, the Westminster police raided Soho and shut down all the illicit, unlicensed sex shops and shows. We believe that it was part of the process of bringing the presence of God, by the Holy Spirit in his people, back into the area.

Graham's first Make Way songs were written soon after a similar march in October 1985, and we used them on a

march through the tower blocks of Lewisham. In the evening
we all got together indoors and recorded the same songs as
an album. That's how the first Make Way album came into
being. The combination of our marching and Graham's
music was very powerful, and proved to be a springboard
into the next phase—a national march.

About the time of the Soho march John Pressdee's friend
Harry Ellison approached him with an idea. Harry was a
member of Ichthus and worked at London's Smithfield meat
market. Harry wanted to organise a Christian event at the
market and was convinced that the owners would agree.

So John and Harry approached the market superintendent
who said yes, a Christian event could be held in the market
one weekend when it would be empty—free of charge.

John and Harry then approached Stephen Maxted, who
had been the Spring Harvest administrator until the previous
year. Together they began to think about ways in which a
Christian festival could be arranged.

Initially it was to be called the 'Festival of the Lamb' (the
pun is obvious, with hindsight) and was to be a Christian
exhibition with an evening celebration. But the sticking
point was the evening event. At that time John was in charge
of monthly celebrations in Ichthus on Saturdays. They were
very well attended as they attracted people from all over
South East London. But the market didn't seem suitable for
a major praise event. Although it covers a large area there
is no central space where five or six thousand people could
gather; the market is just three long, covered roadways.

Harry, John and Stephen, together with Mike Oakes who
was my administrator, made several visits to the market,
but they had reservations about the viability of a Christian
festival, and even considered putting an end to the whole
idea. However, they spent time seeking God and, as they
were praying, John had a vivid picture of thousands of people
starting out at Smithfield and walking round the City of
London, carrying banners, praying, singing and worshipping.

John says, 'The image I had in my mind was Joshua—as
I fell on my knees before God I saw Joshua falling on his

knees before the captain of the Lord's army. As he fell, in
my mind I could see Jericho fall. I have always felt that
Jericho fell at the point Joshua got to his knees and said,
"I don't know what to do. I'm supposed to be a strategist
and leading all this, but I don't know what to do, so I'll
become subordinate to the captain."'

Stephen Maxted was thinking along similar lines, that God
was telling them to march around the walls of the City of
London, rather than to hold an event in Smithfield.

That was when we committed ourselves and Ichthus to
the march. Graham's first praise march had already been
released on record; churches around the nation were
beginning to march and—in conjunction with Gerald Coates
whom I've known for years, and Lynn, with whom we already
had contact through the work in Soho—we decided to work
together on an event which would start from Smithfield Meat
Market. It was the beginning of March for Jesus.

We had all sorts of ideas to begin with—but we passed
the concept back to the administrators to let them work it
through. John Pressdee was chairman of the small steering
committee that was set up. He was joined by Harry Ellison,
Mike Oakes, Laurence Singlehurst and, later on, Steve
Clifford representing Gerald from Pioneer.

The whole administration of that Smithfield event was
handled from Stephen Maxted's study in his home, ably
supported by Kit Crowther, his secretary.'

Graham Kendrick was the common factor in the Ichthus
fellowship's evangelism and YWAM's days of prayer. The
son of a Baptist minister, he grew up in London, and had
a first taste of music in evangelism when he formed a rock
band with his brother and sister.

Looking back at the roots of music, evangelism and
marching in his ministry, Graham says:

'When we started the band it had become popular for
Christians to use the pop music of the day to communicate
their faith. Many churches had converted halls into coffee

bars. Bands like ours were used as bait to get people off the streets.

When I went off to teacher training college at the end of the sixties, I didn't really know what I wanted to do. But I always had a sense of destiny and knew there was something God wanted me to do. Teacher training gave me a good grounding in communications: standing in front of a bunch of people who didn't really want to listen and trying to communicate with them!

When I left college I took to the road in an old Ford Escort van with a second-hand, 50-watt PA. I was one of the first Christian musicians to go out full time; it was very unusual and not always understood by churches.

Even in those days I depended on friendships. Clive Calver, who now heads up Britain's Evangelical Alliance, was just out of Bible College and was a travelling evangelist. Neither of us felt happy about 'lone ranger evangelists' who would ride into town, shoot up a few unbelievers and ride out again, sometimes leaving a mess behind them. We thought it would be better to have a team. So we contacted all our like-minded friends and for two-and-a-half years ten of us, aged seventeen to twenty-four, travelled the country offering ourselves to churches to do coffee bars and evangelistic events. It was a miracle we survived as we had no visible means of support.

When I was filled with the Spirit God began to open me up as a worshipper. Out of that flowed new worship songs as I learned to express worship on a level I hadn't experienced before. In those early days I found many of the new songs rather light-weight and even banal. But I couldn't deny that something was happening when we sang them. There was a new dimension of worship which somehow these choruses, with all their weaknesses, were allowing to happen. My response, as a songwriter, was to try to improve the quality of the songs without losing the spiritual impact they were having.

I became musical director for British Youth For Christ in 1976. In 1978, when BYFC and *Buzz* magazine launched

Spring Harvest, there was a need and a platform for new songs. That accelerated the songwriting process, and my role as a worship leader developed.

At the end of the seventies we moved to York where we were based at St Michael-le-Belfrey, one of the centres of Anglican renewal. Partnership with mime artist Geoffrey Stevenson brought a different dimension to my concert work, but I reached a crisis point around 1983 when it became obvious that I couldn't do justice to both the concert performance side of my work and the worship side. I had to choose between the two. I felt I should concentrate on praise and worship and have hardly done a concert since.

For me the March for Jesus concept emerged out of my exploration of worship and my experience as a worship leader. As I discussed worship experiences with other people in the early eighties, I found that many Christian groups were discovering a great rise of faith or sense of spiritual breakthrough as a result of praise that proclaimed truth.

I became interested in the dynamics of praise and in its relation to prayer and spiritual warfare. After comparing notes with lots of people, I became convinced that God often releases his power as his people praise. For me it was an emerging revelation, although it was actually nothing new.

The next step was a growing question about what might happen if we took this same dynamic of praise out onto the streets. I'd seen that God healed people in meetings when people were praising—without anyone touching them or praying for them, and I wondered, if we praised in the same way on the streets, would unbelievers be healed in the same way?

By then we had moved back to London and, when I heard that my own fellowship, Ichthus, was going to do a praise march through Soho to plant a church there, I knew I must be part of it. It was a very ad hoc affair. We had a big bass drum and a few guitars and one or two flutes. Some instruments just weren't suitable for the open air unamplified. And we went round singing songs that were the regular diet on a Sunday. That confirmed to me that many of the songs we sing indoors aren't suitable outdoors, both in style and content.

Out on the streets you want to declare the truth very precisely, clearly and strongly. We needed specially written songs with a driving rhythm that made it feel it was a momentous occasion. I was planning to record an album anyway and this vision gripped me. As I began to write songs, like 'We believe in God the Father' I felt I should simply declare the truth—for Anglicans it was the familiar words of the creed set to music.

In writing the Make Way albums I have always sought to give the church a musical tool for taking praise, prayer and proclamation onto the streets of our cities and towns. Since Make Way was launched in early 1986 we have seen the vision take hold, with Make Way marches taking place all over the country with different churches and denominations working together.

I see my job as providing churches with resources so that, on any day of the year they deem suitable, they have some musical tools to take out onto the streets. For me that was a specific strategy and the reason I began to multiply Make Way resources. The first 'Make Way Carnival of Praise' ran for a couple of years before I put anything else out. I looked seriously and prayerfully at whether I should ever do another Make Way album. But I felt that the vision was to get the churches into new habits of taking praise on to the streets. If they only had one resource then they would say, 'Well we did that in 1987—what's the next thing?' But if I was to provide them with several, seasonal resources, for Christmas and Easter in particular, then they could take to the streets time and time again. People need variety, but they also need a prophetic focus at different times and seasons.

The resources were there to encourage churches onto the streets. When the Carnival of Praise tape went out, only a few isolated groups were doing praise on the streets. It wasn't even discernible as a growing movement. It was one of those crazy ideas which I felt was inspired by God, so I did it out of obedience. But to my genuine surprise people began to march, and in 1986 and 1987 my office received reports of literally hundreds of Make Way marches. I deliberately put the Make Way resources out in quick succession after that, so the idea could become established.

For me the Soho march was the first push 'over the edge'. It was an embryonic, improvised march, but it taught us a lot and encouraged me to go on to write songs for the streets. One aspect came to light about four years later when I got into conversation with a guy called Greg. I asked how he became a Christian. He had the usual pagan background, and had had some contact with Christians when he was about fifteen years old, but he'd never gone the whole way to become a Christian himself. One evening he and his girlfriend went up to Leicester Square for a night out, when round the corner came a bunch of Christians, singing and worshipping. His girlfriend immediately began to talk them down, saying how stupid they were, but for some reason he felt quite the opposite. In fact, he said that he had a feeling that he ought to be with them. He had quite an argument with his girlfriend that evening, which was probably a surprise to both of them. As a result of that incident he sought out some of the Christians he had known several years before and eventually made a proper commitment to follow the Lord.

I was amazed when he told me. It was encouraging because direct evangelism has never been the primary purpose of the marches. They are much more of a spiritual prayer exercise, but the Spirit of God often does work in direct ways through the marches, touching people's lives. We knew nothing about what was happening to Greg, but that gave us hope that there were lots of other things happening that we didn't know about. As we were praying and praising through the streets, the Spirit of God worked in people's lives. That encouraged us to go on.'

2

The City March

The stage was set. Friendships had been established. The opportunity for us to use Smithfield Market had arisen and was too good to ignore. The Ichthus Fellowship, YWAM and Pioneer had agreed to spend a day together focusing prayer on the City of London. Graham Kendrick was to play a key role using some of the Make Way music to lead the praise through the streets. But major events don't happen without planning, preparation and publicity.

The date was set for Bank Holiday Saturday 23rd May 1987 and the first planning meeting bringing together Ichthus, Pioneer and YWAM was held on 23rd October 1986 at Ichthus House in South East London. In the same week the much heralded Big Bang took place in the City, leaving the world of high finance in a shambles as computers crashed. Yet plans for the May event were not prompted by national news, but a growing conviction that God wanted his people out on the streets, proclaiming Christ in significant seats of power.

In the early stages the event was simply called the Smithfield Project. John Pressdee, one of the Ichthus ministry team, was chairman of the steering group which included: Steve Clifford from Pioneer, representing Gerald Coates; Harry Ellison, from Smithfield Market, a member of the Ichthus fellowship; Russell Grubb, an Ichthus worker and leader of the City Gates fellowship in Soho; Stephen Maxted of Ichthus who had been administrator for Spring

Harvest and was acting as consultant administrator to the group; Mike Oakes, the Ichthus administrator; Laurence Singlehurst of YWAM and Kit Crowther, Stephen Maxted's secretary who became the secretary for the Smithfield group. They were all busy people with other responsibilities. The march was organised in their 'spare' time.

At that first meeting John Pressdee outlined the vision which had been taking shape over the previous six months as he and a few others from the Ichthus fellowship had met and prayed.

The aim was to mobilise Christians to proclaim the name of Jesus in London and to pronounce the defeat of the spiritual forces entrenched in the capital and the heart of the nation. By flooding the City of London with prayer and praise we wanted to express the growing strength of the church and its commitment to the Great Commission.

With that aim in mind the committee set about arranging a structure for the as yet unnamed event. A Council of Reference was suggested to broaden the support base. Individuals were approached to lend their names to the initiative; all, bar one, responded with enthusiasm. We wanted to bring together churches of all denominations and backgrounds to march around the walls of the City of London, then to gather for a celebration rally at the end of the march. Sites for this post-march celebration were discussed. March routes were suggested and a budget drafted.

Even at this early stage there was a very vague suggestion that the event should be followed by a second march through London's West End with the possibility that other cities might catch the vision. But the main emphasis was arranging an event which would focus prayer and spiritual warfare on the City of London. With only seven months between the first main planning meeting and the final event, the task seemed daunting, particularly as, even at that stage, we hoped to attract more than 10,000 marchers, though as plans progressed our expectations decreased as the complexities of planning became more apparent.

One of the main tasks at the outset was to find a site for an end-of-march celebration rally. Steering group members walked the route of the city walls and agreed that the best place to congregate at the end of the march would be in the moat of the Tower of London. We knew we were unlikely to obtain the necessary permission—but that didn't stop us trying. A letter was sent to the Resident Governor of the Tower and negotiations about the route with the City of London Police were set in motion.

An initial meeting with the police seemed to go well. Ideas for the march route were discussed and alternative celebration venues were put forward. But, less then two weeks later, the Chief Superintendent of the City of London Police wrote to say, 'After consideration of all the circumstances, particularly the large numbers of persons involved and the circuitous nature of the route you wish to follow, I am unable in the public interest to agree with your request (to march around the City of London).'

A polite refusal was also received from the Governor of the Tower of London. Other arrangements could be made for the end of the march but we did feel that a march was what God wanted. Undaunted by an initial refusal, a second meeting with the police was arranged for 19th December.

We persevered in prayer. Mike Oakes said, 'We had a very strong sense of the presence of God in the next meeting with the City Police. The initial flat opposition to the march dissolved after about five minutes.'

The major objection of the police was the problem of handling 10,000 people who would be marching in a narrow column around narrow roads in a very small area. They estimated that each marcher needed two yards of space to march in—one yard in front, one yard behind; 10,000 people, four abreast, would occupy a minimum of 5,000 yards—nearly three miles. It would create greater logistic problems than we had reckoned on, so we agreed to modify the march and final rally.

Meanwhile, the march name was agreed as 'The City March' subtitled 'Prayer and Praise in London', and the

various tasks involved in organising this major event were
divided up: march supervisor, chief steward, programme
researcher, site administrator, stage manager, PA co-
ordinator, chief hostess, publicity officer, press officer, music
director, churches co-ordinator. In the run-up to Christmas
individuals were identified for each role and approached.
There was a great deal to be done, but there was a very
good atmosphere at the meetings and a great sense of faith
that the event would be worth all the effort.

Although the venture was new to all of us, we were not
working from scratch. Graham's experience with the Make
Way marches was crucial, as were the Ichthus marches in
Soho and elsewhere, and the YWAM City prayer gatherings.
We also approached organisers of the Birmingham Make
Way events to discover how ten local groups had marched
around the city's twenty-seven mile ring road. Previous
Make Way marches had shown that the maximum number
of people that can march with one band is 250—the band
consisting of a minimum of three brass instruments, one
amplified guitar and a large drum in the middle of the group
plus a lead singer and shout leader. We agreed to alert
church groups to ensure there were sufficient musicians and
group leaders.

In spite of record-breaking low temperatures at the start
of the year, a site meeting was held at Smithfield Market to
anticipate any practical problems—from parking to toilet
facilities. Lists of requirements were drawn up—200 arm-
bands for stewards; twenty-five tabards for chief marshals,
radios, trestle tables, loud hailers and so on.

One dilemma was whether or not to include children. The
day was not an opportunity for a fun family outing; we were
to battle in prayer rather than witnessing to the life and
diversity of the body of Christ. But we did not want to
exclude children or families who could only attend with their
youngsters. In the end we used the advance briefing notes
sent to march participants to highlight the limited toilet
facilities and the extended time people would be expected
to stand. We left the final decision to individuals.

On the national scene the scandal over illegal operations concerning the Guinness take-over of Distillers rocked offices around the City on the eve of a parliamentary debate on insider dealing—another City scandal concerning those who abused privileged financial information to make money from dealing in shares. Summing up the situation *The Economist* newspaper (6th December 1986) said: 'The government is in a fix. On the one hand, Labour politicians accuse it of being unenthusiastic about stamping out City fraud; yet if it starts to tackle the problem with more vigour, the result could be a string of City scandals stretching from now until the general election.'

It was evident that the City—once a citadel of integrity— had become corrupt. Human efforts were unable to change this rotten heart. Prayer was needed.

Prayer was a major feature of the preparations for the City March. Pioneer set up a chain of prayer to focus on the march. Half nights of prayer were started at Smithfield Market bringing together intercessors from four churches. And the steering committee was open to prophetic as well as practical input. One vision given to Barbara Pymm on 6th February was of a black pool: 'The land on each side was raised and hung over the pool. Standing on the raised land were two angels, one each side. They had raised their swords and held them crossed over the black pool. They were commanders, poised for action but waiting for us to give the word to release them and their armies to fight against the principalities and powers over London.'

In the weeks that followed Barbara was again praying about the march and said, 'I saw us as being Joshua's army marching around Jericho. Our strength was the power of God.

'When I looked up the story in Joshua 6, my eye fell on the end of chapter 5 verses 13–15. I was amazed to see described one of the angelic commanders with the sword, just as I had seen two weeks earlier.'

We felt it crucial to pass on the vision to others. Leaders of London churches were invited to St Mark's Kennington on 24th March to hear what was planned, and at the end of March a letter went out to all the London churches on the mailing lists of Pioneer, Ichthus and YWAM, inviting them to join with us on the City March on the 23rd May. London City Mission and the Evangelical Alliance also agreed to contact churches for us. Groups were asked to make their way to Smithfield, praying as they went, using prayer guidelines sent in advance.

Prayer notes on the City, prepared by YWAM researcher Peter Adams for an earlier day of prayer in the City, were revised and updated. These highlighted several areas of influence: churches in the City; some sites of pagan worship; centres of administration like Guildhall and Mansion House, the Lord Mayor's residence; financial institutions like the Bank of England, the Royal Exchange, the Stock Exchange, Lombard Street, and offices of the major world banks; international shipping and trade centres like Lloyd's of London and the Baltic Exchange; legal centres like the Royal Courts of Justice, the Central Criminal Courts and the four Inns of Court; the media in Fleet Street and the surrounding area.

The fine details began falling into place. Byelaws were checked to make sure religious assemblies were not banned—we already knew that they prohibited collections so we could not collect an offering to cover expenses; public liability insurance was taken out for the day; Christian Unions in some of the major City firms were contacted.

By the 10th April 2,000 people had promised to take part in the march and 200 bookings were being received every day at the City March office—alias Stephen Maxted's front room in Forest Hill! We sensed that we were responding to a grassroots movement of ordinary people. Steve Clifford said, 'This was something that was sparking in all of us. We were being blown by the Holy Spirit.'

It was billed as 'a whole morning and afternoon of concerted prayer, worship and praise by thousands of God's people in the very heart of the nation's capital'. Marchers were encouraged to come as church groups, bringing banners and musicians, a prayer leader and a praise leader. Churches were encouraged to learn the Make Way songs which were to be sung en route, interspersed with prayer. Prayer guidelines were issued in advance to encourage everyone to pray as they made their way through London to converge on Smithfield market.

A final dress rehearsal was held on Saturday, 18th April and each church group was asked to send their march co-ordinator, stewards, prayer leader and praise leader. March supervisor Mike Levitton from Pioneer drew on his military background to make the practical arrangements run with clockwork precision: arrival times were staggered; there was space for 4,000 people to assemble in the central aisles of the market known as 'Grand'; up to 2,000 people could assemble in 'East Poultry', and a further 4,000 in 'West Poultry'.

During our planning meetings it had come to light that Mike was once in charge of a tank regiment which he had successfully manoeuvred into a town to find another regiment coming towards them—they managed to block the town for two days. We prayed that our day would bring corruption to a halt—though not the traffic!

The day arrived. Torrential rain poured down as marchers gathered. With such bad weather we thought we would be pleased if only 5,000 turned out. People gathered in the main areas of the meat market. Throughout the week the high roofs of the market sheltered butchers and stall-holders selling poultry and other meat. Now the market was filling up with people of all ages wearing waterproofs and carrying umbrellas as well as church banners.

They assembled between 11am and 12 noon in the three aisles of the market to be led in worship, prayer and praise by a platform party including Graham Kendrick, Lyndon Bowring of Care Trust, contemporary rock band Heartbeat, Floyd McClung of YWAM, Roger and Faith Forster, Gerald Coates, Lynn Green, singer/songwriter Noel Richards of Pioneer, John Pressdee, Lovell Bent, a black church leader, and Christine Leage of the Lydia Fellowship.

At 12.30pm the first group of 100 set off following a one-and-a-quarter mile route mapped in the march programme. Thousands of colourful umbrellas made it a memorable sight. We thought it would take about fifty minutes to get everyone moving and, in total, two hours from the time the first person left Smithfield to the last person arriving at London Wall. In reality it took much longer.

The size of the crowd was overwhelming and the atmosphere was fantastic. Lynn Green and Steve Clifford had the task of staying at the microphone and manning the stage while the marchers left, desperately asking the Lord how we were going to maintain the impetus. The, by now, extremely exhausted musicians were trying to keep the thing going. The estimated fifty minutes turned to two-and-a-half hours!

We kept up a never-ending stream of praise and worship songs, to give encouragement. It was exhausting work, but very exciting. Because they were gathering in the market itself, it was impossible to see how many had arrived. But as they filtered out to start marching we began to realise how many there were—it was an extraordinary sight; many more people took part than we expected. The police estimated the crowd at 15,000 men, women and children.

As well as being encouraged by the numbers, the atmosphere was exhilarating too. It was as if people were oblivious to the rain. There was a tremendous sense of celebration and joy in it all.

Smithfield is not far from Fleet Street—at that time, home of the nation's top daily newspapers. As we began gathering, the noise and the people brought the press down on us trying to get to grips with why so many Christians were marching through the City in the rain. Thousands of people marching had much more impact than our press conference held earlier in the day.

We were quite definite from the outset that the march was not to be a publicity stunt. Our objectives were first and foremost spiritual. We wanted to see a change in the spiritual atmosphere over our country and felt that the City, as the heart of our capital, was strategic in our prayer and action. By marching and praying we were proclaiming the name of Jesus and his righteousness and truth.

Nevertheless we couldn't avoid media attention, otherwise they'd think we were trying to hide something, so a press release was prepared.

The point of visibility is that the church is willing to come out of its cloisters to be counted for God by spiritual powers as well as by earthly powers. We can sit inside our houses, all alone, praying: 'I want the devil to take note.' But the Bible treats human beings as much more concrete than that. What we do with our bodies, and where we place ourselves, gives credence and power to our prayers. So to stand out before the principalities and powers and declare that Jesus is Lord, and they are not, is of as much importance in a prayer and praise march as the fact that we are seen by people.

The response that we were looking for was an effect on the spiritual scene which then could be seen in people: the newspapers beginning to talk differently; the economists beginning to value people as people instead of just by money.

A march script was designed to help participants praise and pray for some of the specific needs of the City of London. Outlining the aims of the day Roger said: 'The objective of the City March is a bold proclamation of Christ in areas which have significance as seats of power. Our togetherness, worship, praise and proclamation of Jesus' name—the word of our witness (Revelation 12:11) are the instruments of priestly warfare against Satan's rule (Revelation 1:6; 2 Chronicles 20: 15–22; Psalm 149). With these instruments we want to influence and have input into the heart of our nation which is the City.

'The economic establishment of the City was at one time considered a citadel of integrity. Scandals of recent years have shown how far the enemy's inroads have eaten into our way of life. Our prayer march is routed past or near many of the City's important markets and buildings. Lloyds occupying the site of the British East India Company 1600–1962; the Baltic Exchange, where half the sales of world shipping are transacted; the London Docks, which contributed in their day to this growth in shipping business, distributing masses of goods produced by the slave trade. Repentance is needed for London's wealth where it has been unjustly gained and its failure at times to welcome immigrants who, for centuries, have flooded into the City.

'The future of dockland with its housing, hi-tech and pleasure industries also needs our prayer. Fleet Street is not far away with its grip on the newspaper world and the far-reaching effects of newsprint on people's lives and values. Many old churches, like St Bride's, will remind us that Christianity in London goes back to Roman times. St Bride was an early-sixth-century Irish missionary, but the site of this church is a Roman house and its excavations have revealed a woman buried in Christian style.

'Bush House at the Aldwych, just west of the City, is not far away and gives us the incentive to pray for broadcasting, since this building houses the BBC World Service and other programmes. London Weekend Television is housed near the National Theatre in the South Bank.

'Within the square mile of the City, London once had more than 100 church buildings. Today for a small population, there are thirty-nine buildings and ten ruins. These churches need to present Christ to the commuting population of the City as well as to serve the needs of the few inhabitants. Let's thank God that St Helen's Bishopsgate is well-known for its evangelical witness. However, like St Paul's and many other churches, it is built on a pagan temple site; reminding us that these alien forces need continued binding and resistance.

'The Stock Exchange and many banks represent what Jesus says can be the alternative god—mammon. We don't wish to see them leading the wild race of consumerism and greed down the Gadarene slope of self-destruction. We need to challenge the spiritual forces that lie behind their wrong use of wealth. The Salvation Army has its headquarters in

Queen Victoria Street—may God raise up more "William Booths" for London and the world!

'Mithraic temple remains are nearby. This god was an early god of the Roman Empire, and was among other things the god of trade. Only the Holy Spirit's power will save us from reverting to his worship.

'Law and justice in our land are represented by Chancery Lane with the Law Society, Gray's Inn, the Royal Courts of Justice and the Old Bailey. Our Law Courts were instituted to administer justice on behalf of God as a gift and stewardship (Genesis 9:5; Romans 13:1–4). If justice is administered as a convenience for man—or some men—we are in danger of losing God's blessing which he wants to give with this gift.

'The corrupting spiritual powers which at one time, no doubt, hovered behind the mystic Knights Templar, who met on the site of the Temple and wielded great power, are only one example of the power bases which have swayed the City and its past and still do.

'Gold and diamond markets are well known, and over their long history have often controlled the City. The Guildhall is the seat of the City's administrative powers. The police (Wood Street Police Station) need our sympathetic and curbing intercession (1 Timothy 2:1–2) as they carry out their difficult responsibilities. So do the power-wielders of more than half the world's foreign exchange, i.e. £80 billion a day, which is transacted in the City; that they may exercise their stewardship of so much of our world's resources in righteousness.

'The plague and the Great Fire of London have been thought by some to be examples of past judgements on the way of life the City represents. Smithfield and the Tower of London, ancient execution sites, remind us of the price many have paid throughout history for a conscience pure before God and a witness to God's truth and Christ's glory.

'We trust that today will be the beginning of a "greater visibility" to the principalities and powers of the manifold wisdom of God found in the lives and praises of God's

people (Ephesians 3:10). To some it will be an introduction
to spiritual warfare, to others the opportunity to do
something positive in the solidarity of God's people to
change the supernatural atmosphere of our country.

'We are not on a ramble, but tackling grave concerns
while seeking to effect serious changes in the heavenlies.
Nevertheless, this will be done in concert and carnival with
our Christ "who always leads us forth in triumph" (2 Cor
2:14).'

The march wound down Farringdon Street, into Ludgate
Hill, past St Paul's and the Bank of England, ending up on
London Wall praying silently or aloud for the people of the
City and against the evil forces of greed, materialism and
corruption. Then the marchers dispersed.

It was a day to mark a fresh concern for City people and
City life; part of an ongoing priority to pray for people and
against the powers that oppose them.

Reports of the day were extremely positive. Local fast-
food restaurants were inundated with singing marchers—in
one, marchers took a collection for the staff. The under-
ground tubes out of the City were full of marchers singing.
Staff at Smithfields were pleased to find that marchers had
taken their litter home with them, and London City Mission
worker Glyn Owen remarked that he felt the heavy
atmosphere in the market had lifted.

Among the 15,000 marchers were members of more than
350 churches from as far away as Cleveland and Devon.
And the event planted a seed in the heart of one platform
guest. YWAM leader Floyd McClung later said, 'It was
wonderful to see Christians come together from so many
churches. It was a prophetic witness to all of society that
Jesus loves England. As I stood there I thought to myself,
"Wouldn't it be wonderful if we could do this in Amsterdam
where I live and in all the other great cities of Europe?"'

One teenage marcher said, 'At first it seemed strange to
be praying at all these huge and ancient buildings in the
rain. But we soon began to feel that God really was able to
work through our prayers; that we were helping the battle

for London by breaking down barriers and repenting of the capital's sin.

'There was such a feeling of being on the winning side. Even in the large crowd, God felt very close and very powerful.'

Summing up the day Steve Clifford said, 'You felt you were part of a grassroots movement. There was that sense of privilege in being included in something that was far bigger than any of us. I felt that there was something unique about the unity of the organisations—that there was an ease of working together and a foundation of trust between us— any disagreements were sorted out easily.'

We learned from the march that groups without a strong leader seemed to flag and at some points motivation was lacking. Even more specific prayer guidelines would have helped, and more scripting with more shouts would have kept momentum going. When the script and songs were not used the march degenerated to chatting and sight-seeing.

Graham Kendrick was the only musician in London Wall to receive the marchers and, due to a planning hiccup, had to improvise with one guitarist, one trombone player, a trumpeter and a bass drummer. In the end he led twenty short celebrations instead of the five planned, as marchers did not arrive as quickly as anticipated.

For Graham it was another practical lesson in preparing music for use on the streets: 'I could see that creative development, under the Holy Spirit, can significantly improve the quality of each individual contribution and therefore the overall effectiveness of the march.'

From that experience Graham went on to develop further the concept of praise/prayer processions and launched Make Way Two in 1988.

Quite apart from the lessons learned, it was a terrific day even though the rain was pouring down. Just by being together, people were excited by the fact that so many other Christians were willing to take time out to come to march. Families were there; people in wheelchairs; people of all ages. It was an inspiration to be involved, as one family,

expressing our love for the Lord and wanting to see the
nation changed through prayer.

We were sure that God would answer our prayers, but
we didn't know how. We were not particularly targeting
the Stock Market; we just vaguely knew that the money
situation in the country was a false one. We knew it needed
shaking up. But whether it would be financial shaking, or
whether one hundred John Wesleys would rise up because,
as we passed the site of Wesley's conversion, we had asked
God to move again in revival power, we did not know.

Within six months the City had experienced Black
Monday (19th October 1987) when shares crashed in London
and New York. At a stroke £50 billion was wiped off City
stock values and by the end of the week they had dropped
nearly £102 billion. We praised God that changes were
taking place.

That could have been the end of the story. We had
marched and praised and prayed around the financial heart
of the nation. There were no plans to repeat the exercise
elsewhere. Ichthus had begun to plan other evangelistic
initiatives for the following year. Our friendship would
continue—but we had no continuing strategy for marching.

However, that summer Gerald and Roger and his wife
Faith were in the USA, quite independently, but arranged
to have a meal together. That was when the subject of
another march came up. We seemed to have stumbled on
something God was using, so Ichthus' other plans were
shelved. Lynn and Graham readily agreed to join forces
once again, and plans began for a second march—this time
at the political, rather than the economic heart of the capital.
We would march to Westminster.

3

The Westminster March

We wanted to continue praying for London and to keep
people motivated in prayer warfare. Westminster Chapel
was booked for the 27th February 1988 to hold a day of
training, prayer and celebration when we could look to God
to speak to us concerning the Westminster March. We
wanted as many people as possible to be equipped with the
skills necessary for effective prayer and spiritual warfare:
800 people took part.

Joshua 5 was still the leading vision. We had targeted the
centres of money and power; now we had to go on to target
the centres of government.

Plans for the march got underway with a proposed route
from Trafalgar Square to Hyde Park, passing the Ministry
of Defence, Admiralty House, the Houses of Parliament,
Westminster Abbey, Buckingham Palace and Wellington
Barracks.

We knew that the ad hoc organisation for the City March
needed restructuring. Busy people can only be prevailed
upon to work in their spare time for a limited period. We
needed secretarial help from the start of January 1988, and
from November 1987 we planned to have an administrator
working on the planning for at least one day a week.

John Pressdee knew that his primary gifting was visionary
rather than administrative so he handed over the chairmanship of the steering committee to Steve Clifford.

The steering committee was re-formed under Steve's

chairmanship to include Rob Dicken of Pioneer, Mike
Oakes, Graham and John Pressdee from Ichthus, Laurence
Singlehurst, Avril Platt and Paul Miller from YWAM, and
the secretary and administrator Brian Harris who had been
working for evangelist Eric Delve. The Pioneer office above
the garage at Gerald's home in Esher became the centre of
operations.

Financial gifts had been received from individuals taking
part in the City March and from a few individuals who were
asked to sponsor the initiative. These funds were used to
buy computer software.

Once again we began to look for a name—and this time,
after much discussion, we settled on 'March for Jesus—to
the heart of the nation'. Mike Oakes dreamed dreams of
ongoing marches becoming a national event, linked by radio,
then going Europe-wide. No one seemed to take the dreams
seriously. When thoughts of Europe were mooted months
later, it came as a great surprise.

But his vision did trigger a response in the heart of
Australian-born Erica Youngman who had recently arrived
in the UK and was looking for temporary work.

'I'd been working on a mission in Paris for six months as
a short-termer helping out wherever I could fit in, primarily
with evangelism. My goal was to be in Britain for six months,
to spend two months getting some money together, then
some time having a look around before going home. The
Pioneer office said they needed someone to work part time.
I was really excited by the vision. Coming fresh from Europe
I knew how key Britain was. Church leaders in Europe have
a sometimes reluctant recognition that in God's strategy
Britain is key. There are things happening here that aren't
happening yet elsewhere in Europe.

'What I understood about the vision was that getting
British Christians together for the nation was an important
first step.'

Erica was thrown into the preparations for the Westminster
Chapel training day. Meanwhile plans for an end-of-march
gathering in Hyde Park were coming up against the rules

governing events in Royal parks: no collections of money; no musical instruments; no sound amplification; no public speaking outside Speakers' Corner; no assemblies or performances.

It was crunch time. A meeting was arranged between Inspector Devine of New Scotland Yard who was responsible for marches, Steve Clifford and Mike Levitton.

Steve knew it was a crucial meeting: 'My wife and I decided we were going to go up there and pray. So we drove to London with a friend and our two children Jake and Jordan. We held our own March for Jesus along the route we wanted the police to agree to, right through to Hyde Park, praying as we were going. When we got to the park the kids went off to play while we sat and prayed. Then Jake, my four-year-old, came over and said, "When God speaks to you—it's to your heart, isn't it?" Then he added: "God says yes!"

'When we arrived at the meeting in New Scotland Yard later that day, the whole situation turned round within half an hour. Mike and I were astounded.

'After that meeting we met with Inspector Devine and walked the march route, talking about what we were going to do. It was at that point that he asked how many people we were expecting. When I said we anticipated a turn-out of 30,000, he looked at me knowingly and said, "Oh really, Sir?" I knew he didn't believe me.

'From their experience of other optimistic organisers the police divide the numbers of marchers expected by a factor of ten. It's not good news for them if they police a march for 30,000 and only 1,000 turn up. But Inspector Devine was to be even more surprised than we were by the turn-out on the day.'

The final route was settled by March. In contrast to the City March when the streets were virtually deserted, we were to march through the tourist-packed City of Westminster, swollen with supporters on their way to Wembley for an England/Scotland match.

A special sub-committee was set up for 'Effective Prayer'.

Groups with good leaders had been able to sustain prayer throughout the City March, but most needed an increased amount of scripted material. Graham suggested that each column should have its leaders at the front followed by dancers, singers and a band. Between each column, a group of intercessors would pray continually while the momentum of the march was continued by the band.

A small script-writing committee was also set up. After the experience of the City March we agreed that the whole event should be more fully scripted to help people sustain their prayer and focus.

If you've only been told, 'Pray about Government as you go past the Houses of Parliament,' it is easy to end up in a sight-seeing stroll for Jesus if there isn't a script. People sing with the songs, but between songs they just walk along waving their banners. By providing a script we gave people the tools they needed to put the best of themselves into the march. The Westminster March included quite detailed prayer scripts as well as prayers in twos and threes.

Erica, who was part of the script-writing group from 1988, said, 'We began the process of putting the programme together with one or two sessions in prayer. We asked the Lord for scriptures, themes and any prophetic acts that he wanted us to integrate into the programme. Then we sought the Lord for structure. Once we felt as a group that we'd heard from the Lord about the key themes, the content and the structure and any specific sub-themes to include—then it was up to Graham to go away and turn it into a script.

'We did try dividing it up into chunks with different people writing sections, but it didn't work. Different styles and sympathies came through, and it was difficult to turn it into a whole. Also, because each writer was only aware of his or her own section, it would often come out too long and unwieldy. It doesn't work to write by committee.

'We worked hard to avoid any political bias or offence to minority groups. We didn't want to alienate people by treading on their toes unnecessarily. But we knew that March for Jesus would never be acceptable to everyone.'

Work on the Westminster script continued from February to May. By April, forty response forms from an advertising flier had been returned promising only 1,236 marchers! One month to go and we were still making preparations for at least 30,000 marchers to attend. A briefing day was arranged for marshals on the 7th May. By the 13th May response from that initial flier indicated a 36,000 attendance.

As the media often portray Christians as money-grabbing we made a firm decision against taking up an offering, although we didn't know where the finances for the day would come from.

Preparations for the Westminster March took place against national turmoil. We began our preparations as the 1987 General Election returned the Conservatives to power for a third term of office. In the year which followed there was controversy over child abuse in Cleveland; the Hungerford massacre when gunman Michael Ryan killed sixteen people; a hurricane in southern Britain which felled an estimated 15 million trees; the Enniskillen Remembrance Day bombing when eleven were killed; the death of thirty-one people in an escalator fire at London's King's Cross station; Black Monday in the City when share prices tumbled; plus Government wrangling over the abolition of domestic rates and the introduction of the new poll tax.

When the 21st May finally arrived the sun was shining. We held a press reception on a pleasure launch moored next to the Embankment, then made our way onto the stage which was constructed from two lorries parked up against each other.

People began to gather from about 10.45am. The police only closed off one carriageway of the Embankment at first. They were still convinced that we'd only have a couple of thousand marchers and they thought they would be able to leave the other carriageway open.

But soon we began to see the people coming across the bridges over the Thames. Everyone had to join the march at the Waterloo Bridge end of the Embankment; the front of the march was further west, up the river at the Hungerford

Footbridge. Mike Levitton had again arranged a staggered approach, so some people arrived at 10.45am, some at 11am and still more at 11.15am. From the stage we could see people pouring over Waterloo Bridge, some in fancy dress, others carrying brightly coloured banners or balloons. They lined up along the single carriageway. Then the police were forced to close the second carriageway, and still crowds and crowds were coming over the bridges. They began to wave and dance. There was a tremendous carnival atmosphere. It was warm and people were enjoying themselves.

We began to realise how many people were arriving when we heard it took somebody half an hour to get from the bottom of Charing Cross tube station up to the top because of the massive crowds. The march was forming further and further back along the Embankment. In spite of an elaborate PA system with a complex delay set-up to allow everyone to hear the same thing at the same time, we were afraid that people would get out of earshot.

Gerald said, 'I can remember standing on the stage twenty minutes before it started and the police handed me a message saying, "You've got 40,000 people jamming the dual carriageway." The bridges were full of people coming across like ants.'

Roger was deeply affected by the gathering crowds: 'When we all lined up on the Embankment I really began to believe that we could see the nation re-evangelised. It was not just that the march could affect the nation, although I believe that it can—but that there were enough Christians there who were willing to give one day to get out onto the streets to be counted by heaven and earth, joining hands across the denominational distinctions, saying: "The body of Christ is more important than our denominational structures. As the body of Christ we want to see our nation evangelised and changed."

'Through marching together many people have learned to praise in a more exuberant and virile fashion than they have ever known before. They have learned unity and have enjoyed the presence and the fellowship of other churches.

'They have learned to pray in a different manner; in a freer manner, with their eyes open; looking at things as they go past, putting paid to the idea that prayer must always mean being shut into the darkness in a room.

'Many people were aware of the spiritual warfare that is involved in going into the streets with prayer and praise. They were conscious both of resistance and of release as they went and the change that it was making. A lot of people were beginning to learn that Christianity is a matter of celebration and festivity. They were enjoying it. Whole families were there; they were mixing together; walking together, then sitting down to eat their sandwiches together. The concept is very biblical: three times a year they went up to Jerusalem. On the journey they collected others on the way; that atmosphere of festivity is fundamental to Christianity.

'The early church not only devoted themselves to the Apostles' doctrine, to the breaking of bread and to prayer (Acts 2:42). They "ate together with glad and sincere hearts, praising God and enjoying the favour of all the people" (Acts 2:46–47). There was festivity in the early church; we are rediscovering the fact that church life is great fun—we can enjoy it together.'

By about noon most people were in position. The police now estimated the crowd at 55,000-strong.

Then the march started, with Roger, Gerald and Graham at the front. Lynn and Steve were once again left on the stage to keep momentum going at the back of the march. We walked twelve abreast across both carriageways.

Marching through the historic centre of power in the nation, our prayers were stimulated by the anniversary of John Wesley's conversion. His diary entry for 24th May 1738 said that his heart was 'strangely warmed'. From that point he went on to lead the greatest revival Britain has known, and within fifty years its influence had touched every part of our nation. Wesley's last letter was to William Wilberforce encouraging him in his fight against slavery. Wilberforce and his friends in the 'Clapham Sect' carried the message right to Parliament itself, not only abolishing slavery but seeking in every way to turn the nation back to God and his ways. As we prayed for revival, we asked God to change our nation in this generation.

At the Ministry of Defence with Horseguards Parade ahead and the Admiralty behind, we proclaimed: 'Some trust in chariots and some in horses, but we will trust in the name of the Lord our God!' (Psalm 20:7).

And in twos and threes we prayed: 'Father, thank you that we can put our trust in you more than all the weapons and technology of man. Thank you that whatever happens to our nation or in the world, nothing can separate us from the love of God. Thank you that you are supreme over all the affairs of the world. We pray that all in our nation who live in fear of nuclear war, especially young people, would know Jesus as their future and their hope!'

Outside the Scottish and Welsh offices, we asked God to unite the land as one nation under God, praying by name for the Secretaries of State for Scotland, Wales and Northern Ireland; thanking God for past mercies: 'that when the light of the gospel has grown dim, revivals in Scotland, Wales and Northern Ireland have burst into flames and touched the ends of the earth! Do it again, Lord, yet in greater power!' was our fervent prayer.

As we marched past Downing Street and the heart of the nation's Government, we prayed for the then Prime Minister Mrs Margaret Thatcher 'that she might know that her authority is from God, and that she is first responsible to the King of kings, not to the electorate'.

Roger and Gerald left the march briefly at that point to deliver a statement to 10 Downing Street. Mrs Thatcher had made a speech in the preceding months asking, 'Where is the church?' It was as if we were saying, 'Here we are, we're walking down your street.'

Roger said, 'Because the church is often too nice to make a fuss, and good people remain silent, lots of things are passed through Parliament because of the vociferous noises being made by small minorities. Many Christians' views are just being ignored. So we felt there was a place to say the church is significant and big enough to be taken into account when it comes to making legislation.

'We wanted it to be known that in any true democracy the church should be considered and consulted, if such a large number of people are going to be adequately represented.'

In the letter which we delivered we were careful not to show any particular bias politically, but it was a positive exhortation to the Government to care for the disadvantaged and the poor, underlining the fact that justice and morality are important for the sake of society. It is the duty of the church to remind rulers that they are under God. That very evening in Edinburgh, at the National Assembly of the Church of Scotland, Mrs Thatcher addressed the issues that we were addressing in a major speech. She began, 'Speaking personally as a Christian as well as a politician,' and went on to say:

> Reading recently I came across the starkly simple phrase: 'Christianity is about spiritual redemption, not social reform.'
>
> Sometimes the debate on these matters has become too polarised and given the impression that the two are quite separate.
>
> Most Christians would regard it as their personal duty to help their fellow men and women. They would regard the lives of children as a precious trust. These duties come not from any secular legislation passed by Parliament, but from being a Christian.

She underlined the distinctive marks of Christianity as

> the fundamental right to choose between good and evil; that we were made in God's own image and therefore we are expected to use all our own power of thought and judgement in exercising that choice; and further, if we open our hearts to God, he has promised to work within us. And third, that our Lord Jesus Christ, the Son of God, when faced with his terrible choice and lonely vigil, chose to lay down his life that our sins may be forgiven.

She acknowledged that

> if you try to take the fruits of Christianity without its roots, the fruits will wither.
>
> We must not profess the Christian faith and go to church simply because we want social reforms and benefits or a better standard of behaviour—but because we accept the sanctity of life, the responsibility that comes with freedom and the supreme sacrifice of Christ.

She underlined the basic ties of the family which, she said

> are at the heart of our society and are the very nursery of civic virtue.
>
> It is on the family that we in Government build our own policies for welfare, education and care.

She underlined that

> the only way we can ensure that no one is left without sustenance, help or opportunity, is to have laws to provide for health and education, pensions for the elderly, succour for the sick and disabled.

From the text of the speech given by the Prime Minister, the Rt Hon Margaret Thatcher MP to the General Assembly of the Church of Scotland in Edinburgh on Saturday, 21 May, 1988.

The snippet of March for Jesus broadcast on television the same evening showed Roger saying some of the same things that had been said by Mrs Thatcher earlier in the day.

When Roger and Gerald rejoined the march, Roger said, 'We came in at a point where suddenly the music stopped and everybody began to pray at the same moment. The people standing watching us on the pavement in Whitehall didn't laugh—they didn't speak—they were open-mouthed in amazement and awe. God was there. You could say they could find that sense of awe in most churches—but those people don't go to a church. It was prophetic symbolism, showing that the people of God are a praying people and God is in their midst.'

The march also prayed for the Health Secretary and those in the Health Service:

that in the difficult ethical issues they face, those in the service would stand firm in support of life from conception to natural death.

In Parliament Square we thanked God for our heritage of democratic government and prayed for the Members of Parliament:

that they all should be filled with wisdom, integrity, a love of righteousness and justice, mercy and humility.

We prayed for more godly men and women to be elected to Parliament and for the House of Lords, as the highest court in the land, that they might uphold justice and restrain forces of evil.

Together we proclaimed from Psalm 2:

Therefore you kings, be wise; be warned you judges of the earth. Serve the Lord with trembling hearts. Do homage to the Son of God, lest he be angry and you be destroyed in your way, for his anger can flare up in a moment. But happy are all who take refuge in him.

As we approached Westminster Abbey and Methodist Central Hall, we asked 'that we may experience revival greater even than that which Wesley led'.

Moving on into Victoria Street past the Departments of Employment and Trade and Industry, New Scotland Yard in Whitehall and the Home Office, we prayed

for those who are victims of a society that has gone far from God and his ways; for the long-term unemployed, that they might have hope restored to them; for those who live in substandard housing . . . and for the victims of the violence and permissiveness of our society.

We asked, in Jesus' name

that the destructive effects of sin on the structure of our society might be reversed. Reveal creative ways to deal with the causes of their problems. Raise up vigorous churches to be on the front line in caring and rebuilding society.

Buckingham Gate and Westminster City Hall were the place to focus our prayers on London and its 6·5 million residents. We prayed for schools and churches and particularly about the problem of AIDS:

> Awaken us to its horrors and break our complacency. Give your people compassion for the victims of this disease; bring into being through the churches many initiatives in caring and prevention, inspired by the Holy Spirit. Restore relationships of love and faithfulness and bring a new respect for marriage, especially among those now approaching adulthood. Save us from self-righteousness and apathy. Let this be an age when your church realises its destiny to serve with sacrificial love and supernatural power. As Jesus served the outcasts of his day, let us show his love to all those whom the world rejects. Let the cross of Christ be lifted up in the midst of suffering, and let countless men and women be drawn to him.

Our prayers outside Westminster Cathedral focused on the steadfast witness of the Roman Catholic Church to the value of human life before birth, and their opposition to abortion. We thanked God for David Alton MP and others who had fought for the unborn child, and we prayed for right legislation to restrict embryo experimentation and use of foetal tissue for 'spare-part surgery'.

As one voice we said,

> In the name of Jesus we oppose the spiritual forces that cause the destruction of life in our land. We ask, Lord, that you would restrain the activities of godless men and women. We thank you, Lord Jesus, that in being born as a man you affirmed the value of human life from conception. Cause us to recognise the sanctity of human life in our attitudes, our behaviour and laws.

As we passed the Cathedral we proclaimed together three times the words written in Latin on the building: 'Lord Jesus, King and Redeemer, you have saved us by your blood!'

And we prayed for Roman Catholics in our nation:

Move among their churches by the power of your Holy Spirit
in a fresh revelation of Jesus as the Way, the Truth and the
Life, and bring many into a living relationship with you as
personal Saviour.

Passing BP House prompted prayers about London's role
at the centre of international trade, finance, travel and
culture:

We recognise that we have all too often abused that privilege
and have not acted responsibly towards other nations. We
are truly sorry for the misery, the poverty, the death that
our pride and greed have caused throughout the world. We
would ask your forgiveness and for the opportunity for the
United Kingdom to be a blessing to others in the world.

We prayed specifically for the multi-national companies with
offices in the area: Esso, Mobil, Shell, BP, British
Associated Tobacco and the arms exporters, that righteousness and justice would prevail in their trading.
    And as we passed embassies and high commissions we
prayed against

the activities of violent men who would use certain embassies
and trade delegations as centres for destruction, and for the
uncovering of the subversive activities of those who seek to
plunge the world into chaos against the will of God.

As we thanked God for the ease of transport from London
to the rest of the world we said,

We thank you for all who have gone out from here in the
past. We proclaim together that the days of decline in
missionary activity are over. We pray that many thousands
will go in the remaining years of this century in the name of
Jesus.

Marching along the boundary of Buckingham Palace
gardens prompted us to pray for the Royal family. Then
finally, as we turned past Constitution Arch at Hyde Park
Corner, march musicians let out a fanfare to start the Make
Way—Shine Jesus Shine procession.

One man saw us and marched along with us to Hyde Park. Then he sat down and shared our sandwiches. He was in that common trap: he couldn't get work without a place to live, and couldn't get a place to live without work. Ichthus have a place on the edge of Soho where we could give him a bed. He went to live there and became a Christian. That was one remarkable result of the day, but hundreds of other people stopped to watch or stopped us to ask questions.

When Steve and Lynn arrived at the end of the march in Hyde Park they expected to see people march past a small band on a lorry, which was all we were allowed in the Royal park. Instead people were sitting down. There was impromptu worship and prayer taking place. People didn't want to leave—so we continued the programme, even interviewing the policeman who was in charge on the day. There was an excellent atmosphere. When we left we were absolutely exhausted—but we had a tremendous sense that something had happened that day. When you see 55,000 people on the streets, you know God is doing something.

Looking back, Graham said: 'It was miles of smiles as you looked down the Embankment. There was such joy and excitement. I was overwhelmed by it.

'Then going through the significant areas past the Ministry of Defence, Whitehall, Downing Street and Parliament, praying what we were praying and singing what we were singing, was an experience I'll never forget.

'Temperamentally I am a low-key, laid-back person so I don't always take in the full significance of something at the time. But when I step back and look, I see an international movement of Christians on the streets that has emerged in just five years. It is incredible what has happened with relatively little promotion and a shoe-string budget. It has to be attributed to the fact that the Spirit of God has put it in the hearts of thousands and thousands of ordinary Christians that this is what they should do.

'It has been much more of a people movement than a leader movement. We have broadcast a concept and the concept has grabbed people. They have not unified around leaders or personalities. They have unified around a vision. They certainly haven't unified around me as a personality because I'm not the kind of person to get up and address thousands of people. But people have identified with the vision because the Spirit of God is saying the same thing in their hearts.'

4
The Torch March

Between the '87 City and '88 Westminster marches we held a training day at Westminster Chapel on the 27th February 1988. (The minister at Wesminster Chapel is RT Kendall, one of the March for Jesus Council of Reference.) During the tea break Graham, Laurence Singlehurst, Steve Clifford and John Pressdee were sitting in RT Kendall's office, joking and laughing. John had been putting on weight and, at forty-seven, had taken up walking to get fit. As we were clowning around he said he was thinking about walking from John O'Groats to Land's End.

He recalls, 'I was just joking with the guys. We were all laughing and Steve suddenly said, "I think God wants you to walk from John O'Groats to Land's End and do a prayerwalk." At that point Laurence Singlehurst started jumping up and down saying "I've got it! I've got it!"'

YWAM had launched Target 2000: the Great Commission Torch Run on the Mount of Olives in Jerusalem on Easter Sunday, 3rd April 1988, to link the church in all nations of the world in a major thrust towards the completion of the Great Commission. That first flaming torch was run to Ben Gurion Airport where additional torches were lit and flown to every continent. Tens of thousands of young people were running throughout the world to symbolise the spread of the gospel to the ends of the earth. As they went, outreach programmes and special evangelistic events were being held to spread the Good News further.

56

The Torch Run had not yet found expression in YWAM's work in the UK. But suddenly it slotted into place. We could walk the length of the land carrying torches all the way, linking with the Torch Run flame-bearers and their evangelism among young people.

What began as a joke rapidly took shape, particularly when Graham asked, 'Did you know that I've been thinking we should do a prayerwalk from John O'Groats to Land's End?'

Graham said later, 'My first thoughts of a north-south prayerwalk came in the context of a prayer meeting. I began to see in my imagination a Make Way march from John O'Groats to Land's End. This was probably back in 1986.

'When I began to think about the practicalities, I realised that a march singing songs would not work. It is not possible to sustain a group on a praise march for hundreds of miles; we'd all have laryngitis after the second day! But I began to talk to people like John Pressdee who were thinking through the notion of prayerwalking. As we began to discuss various ideas, a plan began to emerge. You couldn't sing all day, but you could pray.

'Also to have a large group of people would be overwhelmingly difficult. If several hundred people took part you would get into serious problems holding up the traffic—so it seemed more appropriate to use a dedicated smaller group of people who would walk and pray; a more low-key event—not a big public one carrying banners—but a prayer exercise.

'I remember I was in the USA in the summer of 1987 and was combining prayer and exercise by going off early in the morning. I found a running track near where I was staying and on several mornings I went out, jogged and prayed. Again the whole vision returned of walking and praying in England. It was one of those moments when you feel God drop something into your heart. I had faith that we would do it from that point.'

As Graham's dreams, Steve's joking suggestion and John's prayer and fitness programme came together, the

aims of the event were soon crystallised into three main
areas.

Primarily the Torch March was to be a prayer, praise and
witness walk, involving church leaders from all denominations who have a vision for a major revival of Christianity
and for God's righteousness and justice to prevail in the
UK. Plans were laid to cover the length of Britain in three
sections: John O'Groats to Edinburgh, Edinburgh to
London, and Land's End to London. It was to symbolise
the desire to see the gospel preached across the nation, and
to see a sovereign move of the Holy Spirit bringing tens of
thousands of ordinary people to repentance and faith in
Christ.

Secondly, the Torch March was designed to be a national
prayer focus during the months leading up to the national
day of March for Jesus on the 16th September 1989. The
map of the nation was to be divided into twenty-mile bands,
east to west, so that every band would be prayed for as the
march progressed down the country, covering twenty miles
each day. A prayer diary would focus on key issues,
especially the vision for a spiritual awakening in the land.
As we passed through each region, local Christians would
join in concerted prayer while their leaders represented them
on the Torch March.

Thirdly, the Torch March provided the backbone for the
Torch Run—a worldwide initiative linking young people as
they ran from town to town, village to village and city to
city carrying a flame symbolising the gospel. As the flame
arrived in each area the runners and local young people
would join forces to share their faith through a variety of
evangelistic activities.

We felt that the Torch March was a unique and historic
opportunity to express the unity and solidarity of God's
people regardless of denomination, tradition, culture and
race. It was to be a chance humbly to call upon God for a
massive turning to him in the land through confession,
prayer, witness, proclamation and demonstration of oneness
in Christ under the authority of the Scriptures.

In his letter inviting Christians from across the country
to join the Torch March John Pressdee said, 'I am excited
by the march because it presents a unique opportunity for
ordinary people, who for years have been passive spectators
without a voice, to become a vehicle for the power of God.

'It is my conviction that evil spiritual forces would like
to tear our nation to shreds, but they are held back by the
mass of ordinary Christians who love God and do not realise
their potential in the Lord Jesus, as they hold back the
powers of darkness by their daily decision to live for Christ.

'The battle is on—Jesus alone is the answer to the crisis
in our nation, and if we are to see enemy strongholds fall,
we need a fresh vision of the risen Christ as the "Captain
of the armies of heaven" as we seek for his lordship and
his righteousness to be established.'

John Pressdee headed the sub-committee which organised
the Torch March. He was joined by Graham, John
Adlington and John Houghton, an East Sussex church
leader who has since co-authored a book with Graham called
Prayerwalking (Kingsway 1990).

Months of preparation and training—both for walking
and praying—went into the planning of the Torch March.
Routes were plotted and replotted—major roads were more
direct but minor roads were safer, quieter and more
conducive for prayer; accommodation was arranged; back-
up teams of cooks and drivers were enlisted; contact was
made with church leaders and youth groups along the march
route. It was an enormous logistical exercise, but finally all
the arrangements were made.

A YWAM team started the first leg of the March from
John O'Groats to Edinburgh on the 31st July. Train driver
Jim Woodrow, Edinburgh's March for Jesus organiser,
carried the Olympic-style torch into sixteen towns on his
section of the journey from Inverness to Edinburgh. Jim,
who was on his own for a good part of his 280–mile journey,
took part in evangelistic celebrations on several evenings
on the march and said, 'I've been really encouraged by
meeting people and seeing what God is doing in the north

of Scotland. Well over a hundred people became Christians during the walk.'

The main Torch March team, including Graham and Roger, picked up the flame on the 24th August, and started their leg of the March with a celebration and open-air communion. The next day they set off on their twenty-one day, 480-mile walk to London. Seven days later a second team set off from Land's End, Britain's southern-most tip, to walk to a meeting point in London on the 16th September—the day of the first national March for Jesus.

As the Torch March progressed through the country Torch Runners met them and picked up the flame—a flame which had been lit from the original torch set alight on the Mount of Olives.

Graham said, 'I flew with John Houghton up to Edinburgh to start the middle section of the prayerwalk. It took us an hour to fly and we knew it was going to take us three weeks to walk back. That was quite a moment of facing up to stark reality. I don't think any of us knew what we were letting ourselves in for. We didn't have any experience of what we were about to do. Could we cope with walking twenty-four miles a day for twenty-one days? Could we pray for up to eight hours a day? Very few of us had done anything like it before, so there were lots of unknowns. But we did it.

'As we settled into life at walking pace we became aware of the almost insane rush of our "ordinary" lifestyles. We were close to the country. There was time for one another and time for God.'

However, the march was not without its hiccups. On the second night out of Edinburgh the prayerwalkers bedded down for the night in a school. The torch flames were left burning as we slept. But the next morning the flames had been snuffed out. The school caretaker arrived shortly after we discovered the calamity to say he had found some lights on when he did his last round so he'd put them out for us— not wanting to disturb our well-earned rest.

At this point there was panic. We felt that it was important to maintain integrity and carry the original Mount of Olives flame rather than relight the torches with a match. So a desperate search began to find a group who had lit their torch from the original flame. Eventually we found a Scottish YWAM group who still had the flame, so an emergency trip was arranged to rendezvous with the group carrying the flame so we could relight our torches. We were then able to set off once again, carrying our torches and praying as we went.

The first five days were the most difficult. It poured with rain on the third day; extremely bad news for our feet! Then a friendly church gave us all a dose of food-poisoning. But we staggered on, and after surviving that key fifth day, we were set for the rest of the journey to London.

In their book John Houghton and Graham recalled their feelings from the march:

It's an odd feeling, doing something special, different, while life bustles on in its normal fashion all around. Here we are, striding through busy towns and cities, pacing long dusty roads, while cars and lorries hurtle about their business with no more than a curious glance at our fluorescent jackets and determined faces, and yet we feel involved in one of the most significant projects any of us has ever undertaken.

Groups of people join us on the way, all motivated and inspired by the burden to pray for the nation. They are marvellous, feeding us with local information, encouraging us in our endeavour and even on occasion washing our weary feet! They feel something significant is happening.

One Christian lady out shopping in East Birmingham who knows nothing of our coming, suddenly feels God say to her that something of spiritual importance is happening nearby. She jumps in the car and drives around until she finds our team. A few more minutes and we would be gone, but our prayers have made an impact.

Our overriding cry was for a great spiritual awakening across the land. We also prayed for unity among leaders in the body of Christ, the release of a new wave of young preachers, that holiness would become fashionable among teenagers, for the lifting of the economic hardship affecting ordinary people, and the nation's children.

On the Land's End leg of the Torch March, the prayerwalkers were prompted to pray about church leadership. Ian Traynar, of the Christian Music Association, who led the core team said, 'We felt as we walked that God spoke to us about the nation. What he said can be summed up in one statement: "God wants to do something very special in our nation, but it is being held up because Christian leaders are not prepared or united. He calls them to turn their backs on unbelief and let the fear of God dispel their fear of men. He calls them, urgently, to come together across the nation, and in regions, to seek his face and wait for his word."'

Phil Rees, an Anglican clergyman now working in the Ichthus structures, was also one of the core prayerwalking team. He added: 'The lesson the Lord wanted to teach us through the march was to indicate the disunity and fragmentation of the church. Everywhere we came upon the same feature, and we were aware of how parochial the thinking was. If this is to be changed it must be by a change in the hearts and minds of leaders, for if the leaders do not change, the church will not.

'The Lord not only showed us the problem but also, in a wonderful way, he gave us the answer. The march was an experience of living with four other church leaders, all very different from me, for up to three weeks, and the Lord developed a real love among us. This was an experience of the agape love that God wants to see in his church. It is desirable that all who love him, and are in church leadership, should begin to "love the brethren" in this way. Then the unity and love of Jesus' prayer in John's Gospel can become real. I missed the other four very much when I got home, and longed that we could be together again.'

The Land's End to London team had not undertaken any long-distance walking before, though they did not suffer from blisters as badly as the Edinburgh-London team. However, Ian developed a serious hip complaint which threatened to halt his progress completely after five days of walking. Miraculously, he was healed overnight and was able to continue.

He said, 'With a major healing of my hip, the Torch March was an unforgettable experience. Praying for so much of the day, sharing the Scriptures, singing songs, chanting as we walked along, may have sounded strange to passers-by, but it certainly revolutionised us.

'One day two of us broke away from the pack and found ourselves about two miles in front. We were walking and praying in silence, until my companion, Archie Ferguson, who is leader of a South London home for handicapped people, started to laugh: "Think of the arrogance and impudence of saying we are marching for Jesus," he said. "We can't do anything for Jesus. We're marching with Jesus!" We suddenly realised, like the two walking to Emmaus (Luke 24: 14–35) that Jesus had been walking with us in a very special way.'

As the prayerwalkers moved through the countryside they were met by young people from different towns and villages who lit a torch to carry back home.

Several prophecies were given during the Torch March. Possibly the most striking, significant prophetic picture came during a time of worship and without any communication between us. First of all John Pressdee began to see a gigantic pair of scales, so enormous that it filled the whole sky.

Graham wrote in the prayer march diary: 'Simultaneously John Houghton was seeing a pair of scales which he'll describe in a minute, but I began to sing a prophetic song which started off as a kind of lament about the wasted lives of people in this nation. The big question mark hanging over these lives was "Will they be wasted? Will there be mourning and sorrow or will there be joy?"

'The whole sense was of lives which could go one way or the other. Then I began to sing the refrain: "Hanging in the balance of our prayers." There was a great sense of pain and lament and yearning in the song. I hadn't said anything and at this stage, neither of the Johns had communicated what they were seeing.'

John was seeing this: '. . . a giant pair of scales, a balance, and the balance was heavily weighed down on one side. It was loaded with blood, guts, excrement, vomit and filth that had spewed over the side. The other scale pan was completely dry, empty and high. Then I saw a teardrop fall and wet that dry scale pan; then another teardrop, and another, until the scale pan slowly filled with tears. As it did so the filth began to slide off the other scale pan and things tipped into a different direction. Then from the pan of tears came forth a river which flowed throughout the land and washed away all the filth and vileness until it was gone.

'Then I saw little white coffins and white crosses and families united together standing there with wan smiles on their faces but sadness too, as they had at last buried that which had been left out to rot in the open. There was a sense that peace had come to the land. The war was over, and though there were casualties and there was sadness, nonetheless there was hope and joy for the future. We felt quite clearly that revival will come out of all this as God's people pray. It will come as we identify, not only with triumph, but also with tears and with suffering, as we feel the heart of God for this nation.'

Several other prophetic pictures were seen and confirmed by different groups as we walked and prayed and significant scriptures were given to us. The story of the four lepers in 2 Kings 7 was highlighted by many who were back home praying for the walkers, including Angus Kinnear, a member of Ichthus and the man responsible for compiling the early Watchman Nee books. This chapter spoke to us all powerfully as the story starts off with the question: 'Why stay here until we die?' We felt that was the question for the church in this country. If we stayed where we were we were going to die. As the lepers had said, 'We're not doing right. This is a day of good news and we are keeping it to ourselves' (2 Kings 7:9). We felt as individuals we had to do something. If we shut ourselves in to enjoy the blessings of renewal and restoration, we die. But if we take action, moving out against the enemy, look what God can do! We felt that the march was something that we could do to start moving against the enemy.

Kinnear could not have known that there were four of us in the core team of prayerwalkers. At the time when we heard the scripture he gave us, John Houghton had gout, John Adlington and Graham were badly blistered, and John Pressdee's knees were playing up in a bad way. We felt that the shuffling of lepers' ulcerated feet was not dissimilar to our shuffling forward. But we were being preceded by what Kinnear saw as a division of angels going before and clearing out the enemy.

Four separate pictures were given to us of a spinal column. The initial picture from Rob George of Ichthus, a medical consultant, was a spinal column with very damaged nerves so that it wasn't receiving messages from the brain. He described it as the effect that multiple sclerosis has on the body. As we were marching 'the spine of the country' we were restoring nerves: we were getting our nerve back; the Spirit of God was nerving us again for battle, and once again the church was beginning to hear clearly from the head.

A similar picture of the spine with damaged nerves, unable to receive messages from the head, was also passed on to us from two members of the Vine Fellowship in Crawley. The vision was further confirmed from prayer meetings at the Hailsham Christian Fellowship: the synapses (places where the nerves transmit messages) which were being healed, were the leaders of the church. We felt there was an urgent need for the Head to be able to speak prophetically, and for the message to get through to all the churches via these leaders. (This was a year before controversy over prophecy emerged in the British church press.)

Coming south of Birmingham and in towards Oxfordshire there was a real sense of change in the spiritual atmosphere. We felt that the south was spiritually very different from the Midlands and the north. We sensed a great danger of

dissipation at that point because of the complacency and
soporific effect of wealth in the south. We had to redouble
our efforts to keep praying.

One of our number had a dry time with the Lord and let
his Bible fall open saying, 'Lord, speak to me.' His Bible
opened in 2 Kings 6 concerning Elijah and his servant, and
Elijah's prayer that God would open his servant's eyes to
see the mighty host fighting on their behalf. Shortly
afterwards Graham and John Houghton were praying
together on the lines of the same prophecy, that their eyes
would be opened.

John Adlington also had a strong sense of angels helping,
especially near Hayes in Middlesex. He said, 'I had a very
strong impression of three very, very large—over sixty-foot
angels, waiting for trouble. They were warriors, ready to
fight the Lord's battle at the right time.'

What John didn't know was that about ten seconds before
he saw the angels John Pressdee had asked the Lord if the
groups could see strong angels. Then, directly after that we
received a phone call—via the mobile phone—from Alex
Buchanan, an intercessor and 'spiritual father' to numerous
church leaders, who had been praying for the prayerwalkers.
When John Pressdee told him that they were becoming more
aware of angels he said that had been his main burden for
us—that we would see the angelic hosts with us.

Thinking about the two major prayer marches coming up
from Land's End and down from John O'Groats, John
Pressdee saw two heavy-duty power cables that were to be
joined on the 16th September, when the walkers converged
on London to light one giant flame. He said, 'There would
be a prophetic coming together of these two prayer power
cables, and the power would begin to flow. As I thought
about that later, I saw it as the powering up of a great
network, not just on a temporary basis, but a whole network
coming alive with current flowing throughout the country;
a little bit like turning on the Blackpool illuminations.'

The 1989 March for Jesus was to take place in forty-
five centres throughout the country, linked by telephone

land-lines. John felt that the network of churches taking part was part of God's plan to create a permanent spiritual 'national grid'.

Summing up John Pressdee said, 'The predominant prayer was for a revelation of the Lord Jesus Christ to be seen across the land and for a new unity in the body of Christ.

'After the thrill of completing a most daunting challenge— praying for eight hours a day for three weeks—we sensed that God had done something through thousands of prayers akin to the dambusters dropping their bombs at the base of the enemy dams, and the prayers—like bombs—were hitting the base of the dam that the enemy has used to stop the church "breaking through". We haven't broken through yet, but by revelation we believe the foundation has been cracked.'

The same vision was confirmed when John Pressdee was in a prayer meeting with one of evangelist Reinhard Bonnke's team who said, 'God gave me a vision for this country of a dam and how that was going to crack under the pressure of the water.'

Also a church passed on a vision, after we'd walked, of twin parapets and a wall and a big crack at the base.

Taking part in the march had a profound effect on the walkers. John Pressdee said, 'As we have been caught up increasingly in the authority of intercessory prayer, those involved in the Torch Marches have decided before God to walk and pray across the land from Anglesey to Lowestoft, thus making the shape of the cross in the country.'

He asked others to join in praying for Britain: 'We see ourselves metaphorically as the feet of the body. Many people throughout the world were praying for us as we walked and prayed through the land. We felt as though we were a visible demonstration of the corporate desire of God's people for revival.'

Graham agreed to take part in the cross-country march as soon as it was suggested. 'I felt that we were taking part in a prophetic act. I had just released the Make Way for the Cross album not many months before, with a sense that an emphasis on the cross was important. So when John Pressdee felt we should go west to east, and in doing that we would describe the shape of a cross over the land, I was in! We did feel it was a significant prophetic act and only God knows what effect it has had.'

Setting out the reasoning behind the prayer marches Roger Forster said, 'Marching is at the heart of biblical Christianity, for Christianity is about a God who is marching through history while taking as many of us with him as he possibly can. Of course the march is first a spiritual one, in which we grow and develop in our obedience to the One who said, "Come follow me!" However, this does not mean that there is no place for actual marching itself. On the contrary, the concrete, outward march is a prophetic symbol and is intimately related to the spiritual advance.

'To illustrate this prophetic principle from the Old Testament, we may take Abraham's literal offering of Isaac which symbolised the coming crucifixion, thus fixing the area in which Jesus would be crucified. In the New Testament, Agabus follows the same principle in Acts 21:11 where he prophesies Paul's imprisonment in a graphic manner using Paul's girdle as a bond, the prophetic symbolism is again intimately related to the fulfilment.

'The Bible is full of marches. Israel marched out of Egypt through the wilderness (Numbers 10); Joshua around Jericho (Joshua 6); Jehoshaphat before Edom, Moab and Ammon (2 Chronicles 20); Nehemiah round the walls of Jerusalem (Nehemiah 12); the exiles returning to Zion with joy on their heads (Isaiah 35:10).

'Even Jesus marched in obedience to his Father. A concrete expression of this was the "freedom march" from Caesarea Philippi to Jerusalem—followed by a great crowd of his disciples in the last months of his life. "He set his face to Jerusalem" (Luke 9:51; 13:22; 17:11; 18:31; 19:28) and as was prophesied, no doubt, about this event: "Therefore have I set my face like a flint" (Isaiah 50:7).

'He led his disciples in a challenge on the metropolis, entrenched in hatred, sin and rebellion, under Caiaphas,

Herod and Pilate. He rode into Jerusalem at the head of a great column of people, and was greeted by a mass movement of the whole city. It threw itself at him, but he destroyed the opposition and all its onslaught in the conflict of Calvary.

'So too the church is moving on to the final victory over all evil, and from time to time equally expresses itself in freedom marches with actual, concrete, prophetic expressions. One day we will ride on to the end of the march, which is the literal meeting with Jesus as he comes again (1 Thessalonians 4:17; Revelation 19:14)—the great march through the heavens.

'It seems that the concrete expression of marching lays hold of ground for God: "I will give you every place where you set your foot" (Joshua 1:3).'

The Torch March opened up a new national phase of March for Jesus. Up to then it was based only in London. The prayerwalk through the length of the land prepared us for a new phase; the first national march in forty-five major cities.

5
March for Jesus Across the Nation

Even before the dust settled after the Westminster March for Jesus, plans were being discussed for a march in other major towns and cities.

The concept was first suggested by Steve Clifford at a meeting in the spring of 1988. We had already agreed to hold the Torch March—a prayer initiative for the nation—but we hadn't decided how the London-based street marching project should develop. At that brain-storming session on the 22nd March 1988 Steve Clifford set out his vision for 'March for Jesus Across the Nation'. It could be, he said, 'a series of synchronised marches and assemblies in twelve or fifteen strategic places throughout the UK, held on the same day. A steering committee would be set up in each locality, linked to a central committee which would provide oversight and vision, unifying the ethos of the march, and overseeing publicity.'

He suggested the weekend before the May Bank Holiday in 1989 as an ideal date. It would be preceded by the Torch March and would cover the UK from the north of Scotland to Land's End. The 1988 Westminster event would provide a model for regional march organisers.

As we thought and prayed about this new concept over the next month it began to become more concrete. By mid-April 1988 we had decided that marches would be held in different regions around the UK on the same day, using the same publicity and content, joined by a telephone land-line.

The central steering committee would provide publicity and march information, the march script and programme, as well as organising the telephone link-up and providing direction to maintain consistent standards and a national feel to the events.

However, the planned date in May clashed with the Football Cup Final and, with at least a dozen marches needing help to get off the ground, we decided to move the date back to September 1989. As soon as the Westminster March was over we got down to detailed planning for March for Jesus Across the Nation; we had sixteen months to put dreams into practice.

The growing momentum of March for Jesus stimulated many ideas; some were successful, others had to be modified, and some died a natural death. But, in every region, the march made a huge impact as Christians from the spectrum of Christian churches came together for a few hours, demonstrating before heaven and earth the love and unity and joy we have in Christ.

To begin the process of turning a London march into synchronised regional marches, a letter was sent to a number of Christian leaders around the country in what we felt were key centres. We had existing working relationships with most of these contacts, though initial thoughts of twelve regional centres expanded to thirty as we listed specific towns on paper. We invited the key leaders to hold a march for Jesus in their area on the 16th September. When the day arrived, forty-five centres from the Shetlands to the Channel Islands held a march.

In the letter, sent in June 1988, we described the 1987 and 1988 marches and said, 'These were not marches of protest, but were days of declaration that Jesus is Lord, and that we are looking for change through prayer, praise and proclamation in the streets.'

We explained that the regional marches would be preceded by large assemblies which would be linked to other assemblies across the nation by a land-line, so that together hundreds of thousands of Christians could be praying,

praising and proclaiming in unison. The assemblies would
then be followed by a march in each centre.

We promised advice on administration, information
packs, publicity materials and co-ordination between
centres, and invited local leaders to catch the vision,
committing themselves to join us on the day.

We all took part in training days which were arranged to
help leaders get to grips with the organisation of a city march.
We had spent more than three years drafting and implement-
ing march plans; we were asking them to grasp all a march
would entail in just one day!

The training days were held in Belfast, Bristol, Brighton,
Glasgow, Lincoln, London and Manchester during May and
June 1989. They were not well attended, but those who did
take part were able to look in detail at what would happen
on the day of the march, the necessary preparation in prayer,
the basics of spiritual warfare, plus suggestions on using the
script, recruiting musicians, stewards and prayer leaders.

Some town co-ordinators were unhappy about bussing
marchers to neighbouring march centres—they wanted an
event in their own area. We were convinced that the marches
should be large; we did not want to dissipate the impact of
the initiatives, so we set a minimum expected attendance at
5,000, though in one or two areas we were finally persuaded
that some people would not travel and smaller marches were
allowed.

There were other difficult decisions to make. A Mormon
group asked to take part in the London march. We did not
have a 'Statement of Faith' for participants to sign, and we
didn't want to make a national policy decision about fringe
groups, but we did meet with the London Mormon chairman
discouraging them from taking part.

Marchers in Canterbury were scheduled to be walking on
the same day as the Canterbury Festival of Faith and the
Environment which was to bring several different faiths
together in pilgrimage and for a conference on the theology
of ecology. Some evangelical groups were taking an active
stand against the event but we were keen not to clash publicly

with the Festival of Faith organisers on this, and negotiated carefully with the Canterbury March for Jesus organisers to ensure that a clash of theology did not erupt on to the streets, detracting from the overall impact of the national March for Jesus initiative.

Although each march had its own distinctives, they were united by the land-line, a specially-written theme song and the common script.

The land-line link-up was a nightmare to organise. A tape was distributed to centres in case the land-link failed—but only one of the forty-five connections was not made on the day. For fifteen minutes, technology linked an estimated 200,000 marches in forty-five regional centres through England, Wales, Scotland and Ireland. With hindsight it might have been too long, but on the day it was thrilling to hear greetings and prayers from London, Edinburgh, Cardiff, Birmingham and Belfast. Together, all 200,000 of us said the Lord's Prayer and read a declaration:

> Almighty God, Maker of heaven and earth; you gave your only Son that all who believe should not perish but have everlasting life. We call on you to pour out your Spirit that the knowledge of the glory of God should cover this land. We believe you are committed to reaching the nations with the Gospel through your people.
>
> We declare our commitment to your Son and his Gospel. We offer ourselves to you to evangelise our islands so that every person shall hear. We choose to engage in strategies to reach every village and every area of our towns and cities with the Good News. Help us, therefore, as an expression of our devotion to your Word, to see your kingdom come and your will done in our lifetime.

As the land-line connection came to an end, marchers up and down the country broke into the theme song written by Graham for March for Jesus Across the Nation. The lyrics communicated the heart of the Torch March and March for Jesus, with the call 'Let the Flame Burn Brighter':

> We'll walk the land with hearts on fire,
> And every step will be a prayer.

Hope is rising, new day dawning,
Sound of singing fills the air.

Two thousand years, and still the flame
Is burning bright across the land.
Hearts are waiting, longing, aching,
For awakening once again.

Chorus
Let the flame burn brighter
In the heart of the darkness
Turning night to glorious day.
Let the song grow louder
As our love grows stronger,
Let it shine! Let it shine!

We'll walk for truth, speak out for love.
In Jesus' name we shall be strong,
To lift the fallen, to save the children,
To fill the nation with your song.

Graham had been given free use of the Abbey Road Recording Studios in London—made famous by the Beatles—to record the song as a single; profits from record sales were to be used to help handicapped children. Although the song summed up the emphasis of the march, our hopes for its success as a pop chart hit were not realised.

Graham said, 'The single was an attempt to sum up the feelings of the marchers and help the world at large to catch the spirit of the event.

'The marches are over in a day, but a song can be around for weeks, months or years and has great potential to explain the event to people. By capturing the spirit of the event, the single could pre-empt people's prejudices and preconceived ideas. They could catch the joy, sense of purpose and vision in the song in a way that could not be communicated by a written statement of intent.'

Though the song reached only number fifty-five in the secular charts—not high enough to give it the air-play and subsequent impact we had hoped for—it is still being sung in churches up and down the country and in other nations, carrying the vision long after other chart-songs of the day have faded into obscurity.

Graham's other major contribution to the 1989 march was the theme of the script which also united the march centres. He recalls: 'I know that there are moments when inspiration has come and I know God has spoken. I remember a steering committee meeting when we were discussing what theme should be woven into the march for the regional centres. We were just brainstorming and praying and the idea of the Lord's Prayer suddenly dropped into my mind. I knew we'd got it.

'Previously we'd built the programme around the landmarks on the route, but with dozens of different cities to write for, we would have needed dozens of different programmes. We still wanted to hold the thing together as a unified event so we needed something which gave each march common ground. The Lord's Prayer was exactly right. We divided it into seven headings and worked out our prayers around those headings.'

As we said, 'Our Father in heaven, hallowed be your name,' we prayed in a call and response format:

May your name be honoured—in our thoughts, words and actions; in our homes, families and friendships; in the life and witness of our local churches, in our schools, colleges, and among teachers; in the life of our local communities; in the life of this nation and among the nations of the world.

The words thundered out like a drum beat as we marched.

As we prayed 'Your kingdom come, your will be done, here on earth as it is in heaven' we asked God to pour out his Spirit on the church with power to take the kingdom and ministry of Jesus to the ends of the earth.

Focusing on the request 'Give us today our daily bread' we thanked God for providing us with such a productive land and for its rich agricultural and mineral resources, and we asked his forgiveness:

Lord, we recognise our failure as guardians of this beautiful planet. We recognise our greed and carelessness, which has upset the balance of nature. Save us from further self-destruction. Stir us to adjust our own lifestyles, and to work vigorously towards a healthy environment for every nation.

Lord, we remember with shame that although there is enough food produced in the world for everyone, millions starve. Forgive us where we have not challenged or changed the economic, political and thought systems that produce and maintain such inequalities. Forgive us where we have failed to displace the spiritual forces of evil that lie behind them.

In praying 'Forgive us our sins, as we also have forgiven those who sin against us,' we paused to pray individually and silently, forgiving specific people by name. And we pronounced a blessing on one another and on those living in the region.

As well as praying for ourselves, 'Lead us not into temptation,' we prayed for brothers and sisters elsewhere who suffer persecution. Then, as we prayed, 'Deliver us from evil' we called on God to have mercy on our nation.

The march reached a climax with the declaration: 'Yours is the kingdom, the power and the glory, for ever and ever. Amen.' Prayer leaders focused our hearts with the words:

We have gathered today in our hundreds of thousands across the nation to pray, to praise, to proclaim, and to march for Jesus; because we love him, and we long for his kingdom, his power and his glory to flood this land and flow to the ends of the earth.

We are now going to unite with one voice to call upon God for a massive outpouring of his Holy Spirit; for a spiritual awakening that will influence every area of society; for salvation, justice and joy to come to millions of people. Let us, as we do this, determine to pay whatever price God requires of us, to make it happen! Now Lord, send your Holy Spirit.

The marches ended with songs of praise, declaration and promise: 'I will build my church', 'God is good', 'Light has dawned that ever shall blaze', culminating with the song:

Shine, Jesus, shine,
Fill this land with the Father's glory;
Blaze, Spirit, blaze,
Set our hearts on fire.
Flow, river, flow,
Flood the nations with grace and mercy;
Send forth your word,
Lord, and let there be light.

In every region marchers were invited to work with us for the future by joining a partnership scheme. We encouraged people to complete the card from the march programme, making a personal commitment to take the gospel to the nation by the year 2000. We hoped that this declaration, made together over the land-link at the start of the marches, would stimulate a commitment to evangelise the whole nation. However, although an estimated 200,000 marchers took part on the day, only 1,049 cards were returned. Part of the problem was that the response process was not easy enough but we had to ask ourselves, 'Is it valid to press on with a goal to reach the nation by the year 2000 without a mandate from the grassroots?'

Although we did not have commitments on paper, we felt the ground-swell of commitment to evangelism. The Billy Graham Mission 89 had involved many people in crusade-style evangelism; many had been actively involved as counsellors and nurture group leaders. People of all denominations had shown a willingness to be involved in evangelism so we agreed to press on towards a national goal.

March for Jesus was gathering pace. By now we were looking ahead to marches in Europe and the possibility of working on the Continent in 1992—the year of European unity, the Olympic Games and Expo '92. We wanted to stimulate the same response from ordinary Christians

nationally as we had seen in London for the first two
marches.

Forward, a sixteen-page free magazine, was the tool
produced to keep people up-to-date with the developing
March for Jesus vision and to encourage everyone to reach
out into their own areas in evangelism. The first issue was
prepared as soon as the '89 march was over and, by the turn
of the year, it was on its way to marchers who had signed
up as a 'March for Jesus partner'.

Until March for Jesus Across the Nation in 1989 we had
been closely involved with all march arrangements. Now it
was out of our hands; we were giving away the vision. Now
some bishops as well as dozens of ministers, elders, vicars
and other church leaders were using the script; hundreds of
worship bands were leading the songs and thousands of
people were taking part—of every colour, age and shape;
the uniting factor was our common creed. It was remarkable
that nationwide, only six areas felt that the national script
did not meet their regional needs: everywhere else, marchers
were singing the same songs, praying the same prayers and
making the same declarations to heaven and earth.

After the experience of the City and Westminster Marches
we had agreed that the whole event should be more fully
scripted to help people sustain their prayer and focus and
avoid the event degenerating into a sight-seeing 'stroll for
Jesus'. The Westminster March had included quite detailed
prayer scripts as well as prayers in twos and threes. We
learned from that experience that small group prayer on the
move doesn't work, so the '89 script was adapted again to
include more call-and-response prayers, shouts, songs and
scripture proclamations. Later the more detailed prayers
were placed in the post-march static assembly.

The reaction on the streets was one of overwhelming
enthusiasm. London was still the largest march, with more
than 25,000 marchers. As Londoners gathered, the Torch
Marches from Land's End and Edinburgh arrived from
different directions with their flaming torches to light a
symbolic, single flame as part of the pre-march ceremony.

It was a memorable moment—though someone had forgotten to turn the gas on under the London torch so there was some delay. It was lit eventually!

Marchers in Belfast enjoyed glorious sunshine for their three-mile, three-hour march through the city centre, along streets which had been bombed by terrorists in the preceding weeks. In their pre-march assembly they prayed for their community, asking God to release those bound by fear. They also prayed against violence and sectarianism and confessed the self-righteousness that had seeped into the church.

In Northern Ireland, where marching is common, March for Jesus struck a very different note. Instead of rows of uniformed marchers led by pipe bands and drummers, March for Jesus was a carnival of colourfully dressed people of all ages—from toddlers in push-chairs to a pensioner wrapped in blankets in a wheelchair. The praise bands, drawn from churches throughout the city, took their places on the backs of five large lorries. As they passed Belfast City Hall where a banner proclaimed: 'Belfast says No' (to the Anglo-Irish agreement), marchers displayed their own banner saying 'Belfast says Yes—to Jesus!'

Jim Thomson, chairman of the Belfast March for Jesus committee said, 'All who took part in the march really enjoyed the day, and so did most of the onlookers. One radio reporter had difficulty finding anyone in the city to give a negative response.

'One of the most encouraging aspects was the diversity of denominational backgrounds from which marchers came. A divided church cannot speak clearly to the world in the way that God wants us to. This is not a structural unity, but a unity of love, purpose and tolerance which comes from a realisation of the mercy and grace of God.'

When one Roman Catholic marcher from Dublin was asked if she was embarrassed to be marching with Protestants she replied: 'We are all the same at the foot of the cross.' And in another display of practical unity in Belfast a Protestant marcher wearing orange and a Catholic marcher wearing green, swapped shirts.

The Bermuda shorts and T-shirts common among Belfast's marchers were swapped for colourful waterproofs and umbrellas in Brighton where the rain hardly stopped, but marchers' enthusiasm was unabated. Praises rang out across the Brighton prom; there were not many onlookers, but the heavenly impact was not lessened by wet weather.

Reports from around the country underlined the memorable effect March for Jesus Across the Nation had on all who took part, and on passers-by. A Southampton marcher said, 'We had a brilliant time . . . and everyone who went came away uplifted and encouraged to share the gospel.' Some onlookers in Southampton grinned and waved at marchers—some even started singing along!

The Glasgow march was described as 'a fabulous day' by march organisers. 'The sun shone, the banners flew and something was done in the hearts of God's people as well as in the city. We intended to finish around 3pm, but the sun and the praise helped us go on until after 4pm with an extended prayer concert.'

Also in Scotland, Alloa marchers reported a singing policeman! One of the officers who helped marshal the crowds was not known to be a Christian, but started singing along with the marchers as he kept the crowds in line. Alloa was one of the smallest marches; with 500 marchers it was one of the exceptions to the 5,000 rule. The nearby town of Stirling had been designated as the march centre, but had been unable to organise an event.

In Truro, a marcher said, 'It was wonderful to see how people enjoyed being together from all different churches.' And a Kent policeman commented, 'This is the happiest and most colourful event I've seen in Canterbury—you should have another one soon.' A marcher on the Canterbury route added, 'Some people couldn't believe it was the church—we were so loud! Others were impressed by the natural, unforced happiness.'

One Edinburgh man wrote to say he and his church were very apprehensive about taking part, but felt a compulsion to do so. He went on to say that they all found it a very uplifting experience and really felt God move in a special way within their church on the day.

Two churches from the Borders region of Scotland attended the Edinburgh march without knowing of the other's involvement. They had never had contact before but, as a result of the march, were planning joint events in the future.

Guernsey marchers reported: 'It was a talking point in the town for weeks. We can't wait for the next one.' And in Glasgow, where the Bishop took part in the march, Christians who had felt marginalised and insignificant said, 'We're bigger than we thought we were. Having a real impact on the city has become conceivable.'

Similar reports came from every area. Marchers realised that the church could have an impact in the nation. For some it was the first time they had taken a public stand as a Christian, for others prayer on the streets about topical issues was new. Some had prayed with people from other churches for the first time; others had realised in a much deeper way what good news the Gospel is—and many were moved into action locally in response to the commitment we made together to reach the nation by the year 2000.

6

Out of the Flames

After March for Jesus Across the Nation we stopped to take stock. Erica Youngman, who had been the key office administrator, returned home to Australia to visit her family; her temporary stay in the UK had become much more permanent than anticipated. When she came back after her holiday, and the work picked up in preparation for the 1990 March for Jesus, we realised that the office team was under severe strain.

A temporary stay in the Pioneer office had lasted two and a half years. Erica had been joined by Melita Poulter at the end of 1989, but financial limits meant no other permanent staff could be taken on; the team relied on part-time volunteers to meet the demands of the work-load. The cramped conditions with up to four people and a noisy photocopier in one room were hampering effective work both for the march team and the Pioneer staff.

In desperation we decided to move the march office to the disused end of a warehouse. This makeshift office, a converted library at Bookham in Surrey, was owned by the county council. Pioneer Ministries were using one end of the building to store and sort goods being collected for Romanian relief. During April teams of volunteers had been sorting, packing and labelling the gifts for Romania. They were due to be shipped out by the end of May. The other end of the building was empty. A coat of paint and some carpet transformed it into the March for Jesus office.

The team moved in after Easter 1990. It was not ideal as Bookham is off the beaten track miles from public transport routes. Staff had to borrow an old mini-bus to get to and from work. Also the telephone was not connected, but they decided to make do with one radio phone rather than delay the move. They were desperate for space to work in.

The office team had just returned from Spring Harvest, a national Christian conference, where they had sought to recruit support for the 1990 event which we were calling March for Jesus Where You Live. Erica was working on the next issue of *Forward* magazine. She recalls: 'All the merchandise and *Forward* magazines had just been brought back from Spring Harvest. That very morning we had unloaded everything, packed it into the warehouse and completed a stock check.

'We were in the office counting all the money that had come from the March for Jesus stand at Spring Harvest and checking out the applications for marches on the office floor. For some reason Neil, one of the volunteers, went outside. When he came back in he said, "Have you got the key to the warehouse—there's a fire in it."

'We couldn't find the key to open the door. Melita and I were running around looking for it—but that key was never found.

'Neil went out again and returned saying: "We'd better vacate the building, guys—the place is really on fire."

'My immediate thought was "I must save the computer records," but a sudden crash in the roof above me seemed to be unmistakable guidance to get out with my life!

'We stood outside watching the building burn—all our records—the names on the mailing list—everything was on computer in the burning building. I felt sick!

'I knew that the enemy was throwing everything he could possibly throw at us; he couldn't do anything worse than this. I kept thinking: "He's set the building on fire. We are so under attack that he's set the building on fire."

'Then I became incredibly calm. So many little difficulties had been building up and making life difficult for us in the office—one thing after another; now the offices were actually burning down. Nothing worse could happen.

'We were safely outside and just stood and prayed; crying out to the Lord that somehow we would get our records out. You can lose all your stock—you can find another building—but if we'd lost our records, it would be the end.

'By the time the fire brigade had arrived there was smoke everywhere. We didn't know until later, but the first thing they did was to run inside and move all the electrical equipment—all the computer gear—into the middle of the room and put sheets over them.

'The fire was still burning at the other end of the building. But it hadn't reached our offices. I was really worried because I thought the roof space was open. That's why the fire spread so quickly between the warehouses—there was no ceiling in that part of the building.

'We were praying the whole time: "God, can you do it? Surely you can do it. Surely, somehow you can get these records out." Then the roof collapsed and we knew the fire was moving along towards our office. Suddenly there was a huge surge of smoke coming out of our end of the roof. I thought: "That's it."

'There was a horrible feeling in the pit of my stomach as I thought of all those records just going up in smoke. There was nothing we could do; just pray. God had to sort it out.

'Then, suddenly, the fire died down and a fireman came over and said: "Do you want to come in and show us what you want us to bring out."

'We had lost everything that was in the warehouse, but none of our furniture or computer equipment was damaged.'

Steve Clifford had been contacted by phone once the fire brigade were on their way. He arrived as the fire was being brought under control. He takes up the story: 'I was sitting in my office when the phone call came through to say: "You'd better get down here quick—it's extremely serious. The firemen have just arrived and the flames are coming through the roof."

'I jumped in the car and thought: 'We've got everything

in there—the literature, the computers, the mailing list." It was only four months before the next march which was due to take place in hundreds of centres round the country.

'I arrived to find firemen with turntable ladders shooting gallons of water on the roof. The staff team were standing in a corner obviously shocked. They were praying when I arrived: "God save the computers."

'Eventually the flames were put out and we were escorted in. Miraculously, although the stores section was decimated, including all the relief goods for Romania, plus our videos, merchandise and printed materials, the fire had reached the offices and stopped. There was smoke damage and some water damage but the firemen's plastic sheets over the computers had protected them. There was a lot of water around, but the computers and all their information were unharmed.

'Even as the firemen were dousing the building down we were carrying all the equipment out of the offices—and having to make drastic arrangements to move it all into an office elsewhere.

'It was traumatic. But, in terms of spiritual warfare, there are key points in every year where we find we are under pressure. The office had just moved into these premises and there was a fair bit of trauma in moving as we were right in the middle of the preparation for the 1990 march. We had difficulties getting phones connected, but had begun to get established. Then the fire broke out. The smoke went through the office so quickly—if the team hadn't got out fast, they could well have been overcome by the smoke.

'It turned out it was a ten-year-old boy who had set fire to the building. He was taken into care and the police gave members of Cobham Christian Fellowship permission to visit his family. The team have prayed for him quite a bit but didn't think it right to make contact.'

In the aftermath of the fire the computers and other office equipment which survived the fire were loaded into a van and the march office was re-established in the Pioneer base in Esher near Cobham. Erica opted to use an empty garage

under the Pioneer office rather than the crowded main
office.

Recalling the crisis she said, 'We all got over it really
quickly, though I know I was in shock. I felt as if my stomach
had dropped out and was working on auto-pilot. I was still
making calm decisions, though I felt numb. We were so
grateful to the Lord that we had not lost our records. We
would cope. We knew that we would be slowed down by
what had happened, but March for Jesus would still be able
to go ahead.'

As news of the fire spread, local people rallied round to
replace the tons of food, clothes and medical supplies which
had been due to go to Romania only two weeks after the
blaze. Cash and gifts flooded in. The relief trip organisers
were able to buy new supplies at cost and were able to leave
on schedule for Romania.

The March for Jesus printers were put to work reprinting
literature. £12,500 worth was lost. And Clive Calver of the
Evangelical Alliance launched an appeal to make up the
loss and to provide new office facilities for the team.

Erica said, 'The response to the fire appeal was an
encouragement. We knew something good was going to
come out of such a disaster. I knew that if Satan was so
panicked that he would do something like that, then God
had something better.

'The crisis eased the tensions and pressure we had felt in
the office. Although we knew things would be difficult they
were much calmer. And we knew that people would pray
for us.'

Cramped office accommodation during the busiest preparation period called for extra grace all round. The March
for Jesus computer was still housed in the Pioneer office
although most of the team worked in the garage below. The
pressure of so many people in such a confined space forced
Rob Dicken, the Pioneer administrator, to move to work
in a friend's outhouse until the march office could finally
move to more permanent premises.

In June the deputy head of a school in Sunbury, who was

a member of the Cobham Christian Fellowship, told us that the school was planning to let premises in the school grounds. They didn't want a commercial business to rent the property, but our style of operations was exactly what they needed.

The building, which has become the March for Jesus office, used to be a computer lab fitted with work benches, a burglar alarm, laminated glass windows and lots of power points. It was built around the turn of the century and was originally part of a children's home. Its high ceilings, old-fashioned cast-iron fireplaces and surrounding playing fields mean it isn't ideal for a business trying to impress customers, but it is fine for March for Jesus.

We moved in at the beginning of August, only six weeks before the 1990 march. Once again the phones weren't connected. We were back to relying on a radio phone with hundreds of march organisers trying to contact us. The new phones were not connected until a week before the march took place. Between March and August our phone number had changed about four times and although the number was re-routed, we suspect that lots of people didn't get through.

However, the worst of the pressure was over. We had new offices, a more permanent team and the prayerful backing of thousands of people as a result of Clive Calver's appeal and the Evangelical Alliance's response to our predicament. Although the final month of preparation called for extra effort all round, we felt confident that God was with us.

7

A Response to the Critics

No new enterprise is ever without its critics. We had been surprised that the national media had given very little coverage to 1989 March for Jesus Across the Nation, but in 1990 we made the headlines. But it was criticism and controversy that dominated the reports.

On the 6th July 1990 eleven evangelical Anglicans from Ealing Parish Church, led by Canon Michael Saward, wrote to the *Church of England Newspaper* urging 'fellow Anglicans to weigh up carefully whether they should identify themselves and their churches with local marches'.

Their concern was that 'a particular (and, we judge, extremist) view of demonology, and a highly tendentious interpretation of "principalities and powers", lies at the heart of the official march theology'. Their concern was based on two articles which had appeared in *Today* magazine.

They explained:

> The first article revealed that the theology which seems to undergird the views of Roger Forster, Gerald Coates and Lynn Green has been set out in a book by Ray Mayhew which sees 'the state, government, culture, law and morality' of our land as having been 'demonised' by powers 'now in rebellion' which 'oppress us' and which have to be completely exorcised. The marches are therefore 'not just marches of witness' but they are aimed at 'reclaiming' these 'demonised' institutions.

As Anglicans we are part of a Christian tradition that has never polarised itself against social institutions in this way. We follow St Paul's declaration that 'the powers-that-be are ordained of God' and our church's relationships with the state and many of society's institutions, while sometimes tense in practice, have never been founded on anything remotely approximating to the 'demonisation' theology.

The following week *CEN* published a response from Lynn as well as a letter from the Revd Martyn Cripps. Mr Cripps stated:

I am involved in the Preston march and none of the information received from headquarters, and none issued locally reads in the terms that concerned Canon Saward.

His letter concluded:

In the end, even if there are differences, I believe it more important to walk alongside brothers in Christ and to publicly proclaim our unity in Christ than to do things separately and so emphasise those differences.

The next issue of *CEN* also included responses from three clergymen, and from Dave Roberts, Editor of *Today* magazine, and from Gerald. One of the three clergymen, the Revd Michael Hawken of St Paul's Ealing, and a member of Ealing's March for Jesus organising committee wrote:

We are planning a march which aims to be a focus for evangelism, prayer for those in local government and other organisations and with particular prayers for children in our area. Many of the churches in Ealing will be taking part, a complete cross-section of churchmanship and denomination. We recognise that many will hold differing views about baptism, church government, church and state etc. etc. What will unite us is our common desire to publicly make Jesus Christ known. 'Christ is preached and therefore we shall rejoice' (Philippians 1:18). What a shame that the parish church in Ealing will not back such a venture.

This led to more widespread coverage in the national press. Ruth Gledhill, religious affairs reporter for *The Times* wrote under the headline: 'Anglicans boycott "demon" marches':

> A nationwide 'march for Jesus' is being boycotted by some Anglicans because of views of some of the marchers on demonology, exorcism and evil spirits. Senior churchmen are concerned that some marchers believe that parts of some cities and certain companies have become 'demonised' and fear that marchers will try to exorcise the 'demons'.

The media were alerted to potential splits and scandals. The *Sunday Times* ran a story headlined: 'Evangelicals fall out over demon-buster', with the by-line 'Roland Howard on a split in the March for Jesus'. He focused on material gleaned from a seminar at the Greenbelt festival. He quoted the Revd Graham Cray, adviser on deliverance ministry for the Diocese of York, and Dave Tomlinson, leader of Holy Joe's, a Brixton church. Graham Cray later told us he had been misquoted and was deeply apologetic for the way in which his comments on spiritual warfare had been worked into the *Sunday Times* story, implying criticism of March for Jesus which he had not intended.

Dave Tomlinson's criticisms were more specific and identified March for Jesus as an exclusively charismatic movement which it is not. He was quoted as expressing concern at the 'triumphalism inherent in recent marches'; and that there was a feeling that the charismatic movement had never quite delivered in terms of supernatural signs and wonders and that this had led people to seek something more dramatic.

Although the *Sunday Times* article acknowledged that churches behind March for Jesus worked hard for the young and the homeless, and were involved in relief and development work overseas, it said,

> March for Jesus has been accused of merely confronting the powerless and lost with their powerlessness. The message is militant and apparently at odds with the sentiments of the New Testament.

On the Wednesday before March for Jesus in 1990, *The Independent* ran a piece entitled: 'When the saints go singing and dancing in'. This article by Martin Wroe chronicled the development of the New Churches and said,

> Many of the leaders, like Mr Coates, have written off the traditional churches and are concentrating on boosting their own numbers.

The article also repeated Michael Saward's criticism that marchers were out to 'cleanse the atmosphere' of demons, and Dave Tomlinson's criticisms that the New Churches leading the marches were unquestioning in their acceptance of 'guru-figures' and 'anti-intellectualism': what he called '"I'm a cabbage for Jesus" mentality'.

Summing up the censure in their pre-march edition the *Church Times* quoted Mrs Marion Mort of the Church of England's Board for Mission and Unity, saying the board had 'strongest reservations' about the march. They also quoted Canon Mark Fitzwilliams, Team Rector of Beaconsfield as saying,

> We find the programme very disturbing. There is too much about demonology; and the tape which came with the programme was even more inflammatory. In my opinion it goes on more about Satan than about Jesus.

He also objected to the tear-off 'statement to Government' included in the programme. He felt that an appeal to Government changed the nature of the march from what he hoped would simply show it was 'fun to be a Christian'.

One of his parishioners was also quoted as saying the text of the march script was 'shot through with anti-abortion messages presented as Christian truth'. He added,

> Its deeply emotive text proclaims that in Britain today, children are equally at risk with the children destroyed by Herod, and that the most dangerous place for a child to be in this land is in its mother's womb.

As well as the major criticism that our demonology was wrong, we were criticised publicly in the press, and more privately by word of mouth, for being anti-abortion, racist, militant rather than meek, triumphalist rather than caring for the poor and under-privileged, for diverting finance from true evangelism and mission, for marching when it had no New Testament precedent, and for being exclusive—only allowing friends to have input into march planning.

Our first response to the criticisms was disappointment that concerns had been aired publicly without coming to us first. Lynn's letter, published in the *Church of England Newspaper*, summed up our feelings:

> I have just read the article which appears under the title 'Jesus March Concern', and frankly I'm shocked. It seems that the 'undersigned' read an article in *Today* magazine which was in no way associated with myself, nor Roger Forster, nor Gerald Coates. Having taken it to accurately represent our theology, they then expressed public concern.
>
> I am sure any of your readers could pinpoint several mistakes in communication and violation of general relationship in the body of Christ in this procedure. We must do better than this if we are going to maintain the unity of the Spirit as commanded in Ephesians 4.

In September, when the national press criticism was at its most fierce, we sent a statement to all national and Christian papers to present our side of the story and, following Martin Wroe's claim that march leaders were critical and intolerant of traditional churches, Gerald wrote to *The Independent* with a correction. In the letter he specifically expressed support for the new Archbishop of Canterbury.

The controversy could not have arisen at a busier time, as the march was about to take place in more than 600 cities, towns and villages nationwide. The day before the march we met for a final board meeting. Suddenly we were inundated with phone calls from the national media. They had read the *Church Times* article with Mrs Mort's criticism and the statement that the march script was 'anti-abortion'.

Radio 4 wanted us to take part in a live interview with Mrs Mort, but we weren't prepared to get into a public debate. March for Jesus is not a pro-life march, it is something entirely different. There were statements within the script on the abortion issue, but we didn't want the march to be hijacked as a pro-life march. Steve was still on the phone at 10.45pm on the night before the march as Radio 4 tried to persuade him to take part in the live debate. Eventually he agreed to give a live interview for use on a Saturday morning programme in response to a pre-recorded interview given by Mrs Mort.

On the day of the march Laurence Singlehurst had a radio phone to answer press queries over the weekend, and Erica Youngman and Dave Brine attended the Clapham march to talk to the media there.

We also wrote both official and personal letters to Michael Saward. In a letter published in the *Church of England Newspaper* Gerald said:

> I was surprised and somewhat saddened to read the letter from Michael Saward and his local church leadership team regarding their understanding of the theology of March for Jesus.
>
> It is a pity that in seeking to draw attention to the theology behind March for Jesus, the local Anglican leadership team focused on an extremist position we do not share. They suggest Ray Mayhew has set out our theology in a book. I am afraid I have not read this book, nor am I aware of its theology.
>
> To be clear, I have addressed many 'secular' forums including Government officials both here in Westminster and overseas. My message, drawn from Romans 13, is that 'God is for you'. God is on the side of all authority, in order that he can get his will done through them. There are of course times when we, as his citizens, and sometimes as the church, have to confront local and national authorities because of their irresponsibility, passive measures or perceived lack of care.
>
> It is in this context that the church is being called to march,

pray and be alerted to these scriptural principles. Indeed it is our prayer that the tide of evil will be stemmed, darkness will be pushed back and the gospel—the ultimate antidote to the works of the devil—will run freely throughout our land in the power of the Holy Spirit.

Our prayer for God's kingdom to come, and his will to be done on earth as it is in heaven, does in necessity engage us all in some sort of spiritual warfare as we have declared war on evil and its source. That should be true of all born-again Christians.

In conclusion, the evangelical church has responded to do three things which will focus on the events of Saturday, September 15 (the day of March for Jesus Where You Live):

1. To demonstrate our unity in the gospel by the visible expression of our love for Christ and one another by marching through our localities in a joyful, prayerful and peaceable procession.

2. To ask God to do what we cannot do in pouring out his Spirit on our towns, cities and villages, bringing both conviction of sin and the need of a Saviour.

3. To confront in our personal lives and as a church the forces of evil. We will do this on the day through prayer, by saying in effect 'enough is enough' and then just as importantly, through the quality of our lives individually and corporately. None of us claims this is an easy route to take, particularly when we are drawing on many traditions and theologies, to say nothing of the eschatology of denominational and so-called non-denominational groupings.

There is no need to burn the house down—never mind warn everybody off—for fear of a potential cockroach.

In response to the criticism that March for Jesus is militant rather than meek, and triumphalist rather than caring for the poor, we do believe that what we do with our bodies, what we do with our voices, what we do with our singing, our worship and our prayers, can bring heaven to a situation, as Jesus lives in the corporate body. But we do not believe and never have believed that this is the sum total of spiritual warfare. That's why we are involved in ACET, the AIDS initiative, and the Jubilee Campaign which campaigns for human rights. That's why we go to help the homeless under the bridges at Waterloo. That's why we challenge the Government on certain issues.

What we are doing in March for Jesus is a proclamation of the gospel which goes alongside social action. Spiritual warfare is feeding the hungry, housing the homeless, caring for the needy; as well as worshipping the Lord and preaching the gospel. As a result people are saved, darkness becomes light, forgiveness and reconciliation take place.

Abraham Lincoln commented, 'The Lord prefers common-looking people. That's why he made so many of them.' March for Jesus is made up of common-looking people. But there's more to these common-looking people than marching just one day a year. The other 364 days they are caring for the youth of our localities. They are caring for people with AIDS and the elderly. They are involved in a wide range of counselling forums and facilities. They are helping to keep people out of prison, hospital, mental institutions; out of debt and out of the courts.

These people are not avoiding getting their hands dirty by having a day of praise and prayer and a little walk round. But daily sacrifice, hard work, occasional disappointment and tiredness are focused in a day of thanksgiving, praise, prayer and unity.

Where we have been condemned for being anti-abortion, Roger says, 'I don't mind being lined as "anti" lots of things, because you cannot be positive for Jesus without being anti-evil. It is almost vacuous to say we're positive for Jesus, and then not imply everything he stood for means he's against the reverse. That is so often the insipid tolerance that is claimed for modern life, and we certainly have nothing to do with that.

'We are positive and believe in human beings. I do not believe that human beings should be executed in the womb. Whether everyone on the march agrees with that or not, I don't know, but I am certainly going to assert that, state it and teach it.'

Then, when critics say we are exclusive, only allowing

friends to have input into march planning, we have to agree:
March for Jesus is not a carefully balanced blend of leaders
chosen to represent each section of the church, fairly and
accurately. We believe it is a movement of God's Spirit and
the emphasis is on relationships based on friendship and
trust. The unity for which Jesus prayed is stated by him to
be modelled on the relationship he had with his Father. That
is a unity of relationships not representatives. It is not
surprising that the Holy Spirit has used our relationships to
build a nationwide team. However there is no exclusion
clause for any denomination or church leader and many
have joined us from various backgrounds, traditions and
streams. Mutual trust has grown with love and co-operation.

(See the Appendix for a more detailed March for Jesus
History and Theology.)

8

March for Jesus Where You Live

While the office fire threatened to destroy March for Jesus, and the media did their part in fanning the flames of criticism, we were flooded with positive responses from church groups wanting to organise a march in 1990. We called it 'March for Jesus Where You Live'. On top of an overwhelming response which led to 602 marches being held, the BBC TV's flag-ship religious programme *Songs of Praise* invited March for Jesus to lead a live Sunday celebration from Leeds Castle as a climax to the weekend of marching country-wide.

After the 1989 marches we wanted March for Jesus to take place in every community with a day focusing on prayer. Organisers were invited to plan evangelistic outreach into their own communities as well as leading marchers in prayer for local needs.

Apart from a few fundamental common factors, local organisers could plan their own initiatives. The key factors uniting all the march centres into a national March for Jesus were: marching on the same day at the same time—Saturday, 16th September from 11am to 2pm; using a common script and the same tape from national organisers to commission the marchers; sharing the same vision—praying for the gospel to have an impact on the nation, and their part of the nation in particular; and focusing on the same uniting symbol—the cross.

The theme of 'Children' was chosen for the 1990 script,

though the emphasis was still on the centrality of Christ's cross. We wanted marchers to be asking 'What kind of a country do we want to give our children? And are our children worth fighting for?'

When the 16th September 1990 finally arrived there were an estimated 200,000 marchers representing 3,000 churches marching for Jesus; 90,000 programmes were sold and 250,000 evangelistic leaflets were distributed. One third of the marches were registered by members of New Churches; one third by traditional denominational churches; the rest did not specify their denomination.

We had support from senior leaders from the Church of England, Baptist, Methodist, Pentecostal and New Churches. George Carey, the Archbishop of Canterbury designate, lent his support. The Bishop of Coventry, Simon Barrington-Ward, who took part in his local march, said, 'In my experience the March for Jesus has provided a wonderful opportunity for Christians of all backgrounds and denominations to come together and to proclaim and demonstrate their faith in a way that has made a real impact on those in the streets of our city.'

From around the country reports flooded into the office of a day which had brought Christians together in a joyful act of witness. Small groups had discovered they could make an impact; larger marches found new links formed between churches who had never worked together before; individuals stood up to be counted for their faith for the first time, and onlookers were delighted to see the church on the move in such a cheerful celebration—some became Christians as a result. In many areas the march marked the start of evangelistic initiatives, and time and again we were asked, 'When can we do this again?'

Not everyone felt enthusiastic at first. As one marcher in Carlisle said: '. . . I cringe from loudness, banners and singing in the streets. But I could not escape the vision of another street procession through an older city than Carlisle. At the centre of it was One who carried a banner of such weight that he collapsed under it. And at the end of that procession his banner carried him while the crowds mocked. If Jesus marched in that procession and carried that banner for me, how could I be ashamed to march for him?'

The unity Jesus prayed for before he went to the cross was a hallmark of many marches. In Belfast, Graham led a massive crowd of 15,000 marchers to Belfast City Hall in the centre of the city for a presentation of 'Make Way for the Cross'. The venue was particularly significant, we were told, as the Ulster covenant had been signed in blood on the same spot. Now we were celebrating the New Covenant, sealed by the blood of Jesus.

Belfast organiser Jim Thompson said Catholics and Protestants walked together on the march: 'We concentrated on the cross—it is the only solution.' The Ulster marchers did not ignore the sectarian issues which continue to divide the province. Jim Thompson said, 'We tailored the script to pray specifically for the problems of Northern Ireland. Basically we were trying to help the church to be honest and real about how we respond to these issues.'

In London fifty-nine marches took place and five converged on Clapham Common where thousands of Christians celebrated their faith with singing, dancing and prayer. It was the biggest march celebration of the day.

Local organiser Pastor Les Ball of Bonneville Christian Centre, said, 'We were praying particularly about the black and white situation. There were many acts of reconciliation as there were both black and white Christians on the march. It was absolutely brilliant to see so many churches standing together. It was a very joyful occasion with literally hundreds of banners.'

In the smaller village marches, several local organisers said that the impact was felt particularly by the Christians taking part as they walked together, ignoring denominational differences.

Children led the way in Thornbury near Bristol where more than 100 youngsters joined 500 adults for a march through the town centre. Four long-term prisoners from Ley Hill Open Prison, accompanied by the assistant prison

chaplain, took a leading role, carrying a cross as the focus
of the march. Terry Wicks, one of the local organisers, said,
'They wanted to come as prisoners—but as Christian
prisoners.' The foursome have come to Christ since their
detention and one carried a banner which read, 'I was in
prison and you visited me.'

Comments reported from the Clitheroe march included:
'When's the next march?' 'Forgive me for doubting the
decision to join the march;' and 'I'm amazed at the size of
the turn-out.' A late decision to join the march meant
organisers had only five weeks to plan the Clitheroe event;
they expected 200 marchers and were amazed to see more
than 250 marchers taking part. Local church unity was
strengthened and the combined church music group which
banded together for the occasion planned to stay in touch
for future events.

Two Russian Orthodox priests took part in the march
through Shipley. Wearing their traditional black robes and
hats, they joined the other 250 marchers from a dozen
churches carrying colourful balloons.

Only two of the seven churches from West Denton,
Newcastle upon Tyne, had any experience of marching.
Their verdict: 'The biggest and best attended "ecumenical"
event in the area. It encouraged local churches to see that
they could do things together. Individuals learned new songs
and people were encouraged to think about activities we
could do together to make Jesus known.' The seven churches
included one United Reformed, one Roman Catholic, three
Anglican, one Methodist church and a Christian fellowship.

Evangelism was a key-note in many areas and in some areas
marchers saw an immediate response to their prayers. In
Eastbourne 500 marchers prayed about the town's suicide
blackspot Beachy Head. One fifty-year-old man who stopped
to watch the march had been to the cliffs that morning
contemplating suicide. He responded to the evangelistic
message at the end of the march and attended a local church
the next day, though has not remained part of the church.

In Lincoln a marcher found a girl in floods of tears in a

public toilet along the march route. She had been convicted by the words said and sung by the 900 marchers; she responded to Christ there and then, and attended church the next day.

Preston's 2,000 Christian marchers gave evangelistic leaflets to Hindu residents who were on their way to the local temple and, at the end of the march, they launched hundreds of helium-filled balloons inviting finders to return the attached label. As well as finding which balloon went furthest, Preston's march organisers sent evangelistic literature to each person who returned a balloon label. Mrs Pamela Cooke, one of the marchers said, 'It was a very moving symbol of our evangelism going further.'

One of the five police officers escorting twin marches in the Nottinghamshire villages of Edwinstone and New Ollerton, visited one of the march organisers after the event to say he had been a member of a church as a teenager, but had not maintained fellowship with a church. The march had moved him to face up to his faith again.

The march helped to publicise the planting of a new church in Kippax, a village on the edge of Leeds. Richard Hind, the leader of the new church said, 'It was a very happy atmosphere as we set off down the main street; a little bit of heaven broke out!' A total of ninety-six people from six churches took part.

In Dewsbury, West Yorkshire, 350 marchers arrived on the Town Hall steps to find a Muslim wedding was taking place inside. One of the march organisers said, 'Many of their children stayed for a full forty-five minutes, taking in everything that was said and sung.'

In Malton, North Yorkshire, a biker tried to drown a marcher's testimony at the march rally by revving his bike engine. A nearby policeman confiscated his keys until the march moved off and, the following Monday morning, the biker asked a work-mate, who was one of the marchers: 'What was it all about?' It was a perfect opportunity to share God's good news.

In the Welsh farming area around Newcastle Emlyn,

thirty-five Christians marched and in nearby Cardigan, fifty marchers took to the streets. Four churches from the two areas were involved and marchers reported that one person became a Christian as a result of the day's events. Marchers said it was 'well worth doing', 'a lot of fun' and 'encouraging in terms of numbers of marchers and public interest'. They followed up the march with an evangelistic event in a local barn led by Don Double during November.

Marchers in the Waterside area of Southampton were drawn from eleven local churches and comprised 180 people—and a donkey! After marching through a local housing estate they held a prayer rally and said the day formed an integral part of their ongoing programme of evangelism in the area. As a result of the march, members of the participating churches had developed closer relationships; the church was made visible and Jesus was exalted.

Eight churches, out of a possible thirty, took part in Maidenhead, Berkshire, but together they mustered around 500 marchers. The event attracted lots of onlookers from the multi-story blocks they passed. One young man responded to an appeal made at the evening event which followed the march; he subsequently made a commitment to Christ and was baptised.

Although there was no land-link, the tape introducing the march, plus the common script, and the fact we were all marching at the same time on the same day, had a unifying impact. Marchers in Erdington, North Birmingham said that being part of something bigger—on a national scale—gave them a greater sense of purpose. The 250 marchers included eleven church leaders with their congregations as well as members from eight other churches. However, one of the march organisers said, 'People are beginning to associate these events with the name of Jesus, rather than with "church", which is very pleasing.'

Prayer was the key to the day for many participants. The Edinburgh march was linked into a four-part, year-long strategy to circle the city, marching and praying from parish to parish. David Hill, one of the Edinburgh march organisers, described it as a 'joyful, positive and audible event'.

On a smaller scale members of St John's Parish Church, Worksop, incorporated parts of the march into a prayer-walking programme they were following, walking round the parish, stopping at each of the schools to pray for staff and pupils. One organiser said, 'We found it very moving. There was a real sense that we were achieving something.'

Taking the walls off the church was a new experience for many marchers and onlookers used to more sedate Sunday worship. Residents of Barrow-in-Furness did not escape with a quiet Saturday—some even complained about the noise as marchers held their prayer assembly. A large cross was carried on a trailer as part of the procession, and as 'Lift High the Cross' was sung, the cross was hoisted into the air, catching the attention of passers-by.

In Truro marchers came close to clashing with war veterans marking Battle of Britain day. They were using a fairground organ to play war-time songs in Truro's main street. March organisers finally reached a compromise when the organist agreed to play the hymn 'O for a Thousand Tongues' as marchers passed on their way to Truro Cathedral. A prayer assembly held outside the cathedral included a presentation by forty children dancing to the song 'Hosanna'.

Marching and praying on the streets was completely new for residents of Market Harborough, Leicestershire, where Dean Austin, one of the organisers said, 'The joyful music and shouts, combined with so much colour with the banners, balloons and children who had dressed up, turned many heads.' Marchers included Baptists, Roman Catholics, Methodists, members of an Evangelical Church, an Abundant Life fellowship and the Jesus Army. The three local Anglican churches declined to join, though individual members did take part. Marchers were also joined by the Leader of the Council. One lady in her mid-sixties came out of a cafe to listen to the singing and said it was as if something pulled her towards the marchers. As she joined the crowd, she was overwhelmed by the sense of joy and love. A Christian lady started talking to her and visited her later in the week when, after explaining the gospel, she led her to Christ. The lady and her husband were in church the next Sunday.

But the controversy before the march had had an impact. Rev Malcolm MacNaughton, Anglican priest-in-charge of All Saints' United Anglican-Methodist Church, Newton Hall, Durham wrote to congratulate March for Jesus 'because it is such a positive and effective celebration, and I want to see it continue as such'.

But he also pointed out that all was not well during the run-up to the event: 'People were either against those who taught a theology of spiritual warfare, or against liberals in the church, or against the Government, and it seemed as if a tremendous opportunity for Christians to get together and march *for* Jesus and be seen to be first and foremost *for* him as he is *for* us, was going to be lost in disunity and disloyalty to him.'

March reports and photographs flooding into the March for Jesus office show that events throughout the country were marked by a sense of unity and purpose as Christians prayed together and committed themselves to caring, prayerful action in their community.

One of the main aims of the march was to pray for children. Throughout the country march leaders using the script announced:

> We are celebrating today the wisdom of God who has chosen the foolish things of this world to shame the wise, and the weak things of this world to shame the strong. We are proclaiming his tender love towards the downtrodden, the defenceless and the exploited, especially the children of the world.
>
> Today we have been united with Christians throughout the land in praise and proclamation. Now we come to cry out to God in prayer for Great Britain and especially its children, and to commit ourselves to reach our community with the gospel.

We are engaged in a fierce spiritual battle—a battle for Britain. The Bible says that our struggle is not against flesh and blood but against spiritual forces of evil in the heavenly realms. Prayer is the church's secret weapon in this struggle. Let's use it to the full as we approach the climax of this great day.

We are a nation under spiritual attack, but we are also a nation under God's righteous judgement. It has been said that if God did not judge the western nations like ours he would have to apologise to Sodom and Gomorrah. Yet God is also a God of mercy and is unwilling that any should perish but rather come to a knowledge of the truth.

Time and again in history God has stirred his servants to cry out as we are doing today, that mercy should triumph over judgement, and that through the preaching of the gospel the course of a nation's history should be changed, as in the days of Wesley and Whitefield.

Scripture says that judgement begins in the house of God. We need to confess and repent of our sins and failures, lament the harm brought to so many lives, and cry out to God for his mercy on the basis of what Jesus did through the cross.

Marchers were then called to pray particularly for children in the world and in the church. The final section of prayer focused on evangelism in Britain, 'that this land is blanketed with the gospel, that every person in our land, whatever their background, hears the gospel of Jesus Christ, and that there is a nationwide turning to God'.

Marchers were also invited to commit themselves 'to reach out with the good news, starting where we live'. Together we repeated the commitment made first in 1989 with the prayer: 'We recognise that you have commanded us to evangelise. Therefore, in obedience, we offer ourselves to you to evangelise our islands so that every person shall hear. We choose to engage in strategies to reach every village and every area of our towns and cities with the good news. Help us, therefore, as an expression of our devotion to you, the King of kings, to see your kingdom come and your will done in our lifetime.'

A Children's Charter was signed in most of the venues as part of the day, calling on the Government to promote justice and freedom for the oppressed, to provide shelter for the homeless and to care for the weak and defenceless—particularly the nation's children. Later in the year 34,000 signed copies of the card were delivered to the Prime Minister at Downing Street.

The climax of the weekend of marching was to have been a live broadcast of a March for Jesus celebration at Leeds Castle on Sunday, 17th September. Church groups from in and around Kent and East London were invited to attend. Everything went as planned, until two minutes into the broadcast. Suddenly an estimated five million viewers were faced with a blank screen.

The 3,500 Christians gathered at Leeds Castle waited with bated breath to see if 'unprecedented technical difficulties' could be overcome, but it was not to be. Engineers only managed to regain control of their equipment as the programme was due to end. It was the first time in twenty-nine years of broadcasting the programme that it had been cancelled due to technical problems. Instead of seeing a live broadcast of March for Jesus, viewers were treated to a re-run of *Songs of Praise* at Spring Harvest.

Explaining what happened, Stephen Whittle, head of religious programmes for the BBC said, 'All the cameras and video tape sources come through a central mixing desk. Two minutes or so into the broadcast it failed to function and it proved impossible to get it repaired until 7.10pm.'

He described the event as 'a technical disaster' and added, 'It was an unexpected technical problem, completely new to all of us involved.'

Martyn Lewis, who presented the programme, was also taken by surprise when the equipment failed, saying he'd never known anything like it in his twenty-three years of broadcasting.

The BBC switchboard was inundated by 150 callers wanting to know more about the problem. The programme was rescheduled two weeks later, at a time when *Songs of*

Praise audiences are known to be much higher than they would have been on the earlier date. At the time it was a huge disappointment—though perhaps not unexpected in a year which had seen so many problems as well as blessings. But in the end nothing was lost.

9

Prayer March Across the Nation

As final preparations were being made for the 1990 March for Jesus, the prayerwalkers were back on the road to complete the shape of the cross over Britain. Abram had been commanded to 'walk the length and breadth of the land' (Genesis 13:17) and we took up the same challenge in completing the task we had begun a year earlier. This time the prayerwalkers were to walk across the nation, 350 miles west to east, from Holyhead to Lowestoft.

The 1990 team was drawn from the two groups who had walked from Edinburgh to London and from Land's End to London. They set off on the 31st August and reached Lowestoft on the 15th September—the day before March for Jesus was due to take place in 600 centres around the country.

During a preparation day held at Ashburnham Place in East Sussex, the walkers focused on the seven sayings of Jesus on the cross. The theme of the cross also emerged on the walk itself, and it was in the course of this prayerwalk that Graham began to write 'Crown Him' based on Psalm 24—a collection of songs for the streets which was later used for the 1991 and 1992 Marches for Jesus. It also became the first praise march album on general release in the United States, rapidly spreading the vision there.

Prayer concerts were a feature of the march across the nation. As we said to those who took part, prayer concerts are not new. Both George Whitefield and Jonathan Edwards used the terms and encouraged all Christians to join in concerts of prayer. John Earwicker of the Evangelical Alliance explains: 'What they had in mind in using the phrase "prayer concerts" is the promise Jesus made in Matthew 18:19–20: "If two of you on earth agree about anything you ask for, it will be done for you by my Father in heaven." The Greek word meaning "agree together" is the word from which we take our word "symphony". Here is the idea of different instruments playing distinctively but harmoniously. So in prayer we can become a symphony —we create a prayer concert.'

The emphasis of these prayer concerts was to pray for spiritual awakening in Britain, but we also prayed for local concerns. On the first night in Holyhead they had visions of doors of revival in Wales opening and the next day in Prestatyn Graham improvised a song based on Psalm 24:7–10, which later became part of the 'Crown Him' collection:

Lift up your heads, O you gates; be lifted up, you ancient doors, that the King of glory may come in.

People wept as 'Here is Love', an old hymn by William Rees, was sung in Welsh:

Here is love vast as the ocean,
Loving kindness as the flood,
When the Prince of life, our ransom,
Shed for us His precious blood.
Who His love will not remember?
Who can cease to sing His praise?
He can never be forgotten
Throughout heaven's eternal days.

On the mount of crucifixion
Fountains opened deep and wide;
Through the floodgates of God's mercy
Flowed a vast and gracious tide.
Grace and love, like mighty rivers,
Poured incessant from above,

And heaven's peace and perfect justice
Kissed a guilty world in love.
(William Rees 1802–1883)

The song was also included in Graham's album *Crown Him*.

Along the way the prayerwalkers were encouraged by
many prophetic words, pictures and signs. A number of
themes were repeated throughout the prayer march: reject-
ing self-pity; caring for the marginalised; and the themes in
Isaiah 61. There was an emphasis on ancient doors opening
as in Psalm 24 and on the impact of unity in the church. In
particular we saw a picture of a sword which was too big
for anyone to pick up alone. All the churches need to work
together to wield it. Similarly we saw a picture of a huge
jug which was full and needed everyone to pull on a rope,
together, to tip it over and fill us all.

As we approached Derby, the point at which the 1990
west-east route crossed the 1989 north-south route, we broke
bread together. That morning John Pressdee received a
phone call from his wife Yvonne to say Harry Ellison—who
had played a key role in the City March—had rung to tell
the prayerwalkers to look up because God was going to
show us something in the sky. Also that morning, as the
walkers gathered to pray before they began the day's walk,
the themes of the cross and the truths of the Trinity were
suggested as prayer targets.

As we reached Derby we did look up and, filling the whole
of the otherwise clear blue sky, was the perfect shape of a
cross made out of aeroplane vapour trails. Not only that,
but the sun was shining precisely at the crux of the cross.
Simultaneously just to the left, also in vapour trails, was a
perfect triangle, the sign of the Trinity. Everyone was so
excited we started running, singing, laughing and praising
God as we watched the cross-shaped cloud floating horizont-
ally over us and gradually disperse. We wept and laughed
as we realised we were caught up in something significant,
though we didn't know what. We were just obeying God
and he was encouraging us in a most unusual manner.

We felt we were a vehicle that was carrying the heart of

God's people in prayer over the country. We broke bread by some traffic lights at a crossroads in Derby a few yards from where our west-east route intercepted the previous year's north-south trek.

God also encouraged individuals. John Pressdee is very keen on old aeroplanes. After the date for the 1990 March had been set, we discovered that we had inadvertently picked the very day that the 50th anniversary of the Battle of Britain was to be commemorated in London. Hence we had dubbed the March 'the Battle *for* Britain'. John was going to miss a spectacular air display as he'd be completing the prayerwalk in East Anglia. But for two days, as we walked through East Anglia, the entire display was rehearsed right over our heads. John had the whole display to himself!

The Battle of Britain had been fought and won in the sky. In the spiritual realm we also felt that the battle was going to be in the heavenlies as well as on the ground. One small aspect of that battle was uncovered as we were walking through East Anglia. We found hundreds of yards of audio tape that had been carefully and neatly tied up along hedgerows around farm land. Probably no one else would have discovered it, as we were walking along paths next to major roads. The tape was not thrown out of cars all higgledy-piggledy, but had been deliberately tied there. It is common practice for some occultists to tape curses onto audio cassettes to curse the land, then tie the tape round the fields, so we ripped the tape out as we walked.

The prayerwalk provided many opportunities for reflection on the whole March for Jesus concept. Graham said, 'We feel that our calling is very much that of John the Baptist: "Prepare the way; build up a highway for the King of kings." There is a sense of heralding his coming, announcing his arrival.'

As we walked and talked of other revivals we felt that March for Jesus should be preparing the way of the Lord; bringing down high places and raising up the valleys so that there would be a clear way for the Lord to come.

That had implications for our thoughts on evangelism and

March for Jesus. Graham said, 'For me the Prayer Across
the Nation March was a time for reassessment, saying:
"What is the heart of March for Jesus? What is it really all
about?"

'My own feeling was that the heart of the event is
honouring Jesus; exalting him in public; proclaiming who
he is; proclaiming his kingdom and praying for his will to
be done on earth. It is all Jesus-centred—getting the whole
body of Christ out on the streets to praise him.

'We became concerned that the March should not become
complicated with other agendas but keep close to the original
vision. I think that was a crucial stage in the development
of March for Jesus. We were in danger of moving away from
what God had asked us to do. But now that the vision is
being caught in other nations, we feel much more confident
that we are staying on track. Praise marching and prayer
events are what God has asked us to do. That is the vision
that people were catching through March for Jesus.

'Once you've got that intact and you've done your march
then there are all kinds of things that can go off the back
of it.' The *March for Jesus Guide to Evangelism* was
produced later to provide churches with ideas to complement
the central vision of March for Jesus.

When we got to Lowestoft on the 15th September we
looked out to Europe and began thinking about 1992 and
plans for European unity. That was when we first began to
formulate plans for a prayerwalk to Europe.

John Pressdee said, 'Watching news of the Channel
Tunnel, when the French and English met, did something
really peculiar in my heart. I felt the Holy Spirit saying: "I
want you to meet French believers on the other side." We
need to repent of our insularity. We want there to be total
revival in Europe.'

In 1991 the prayerwalkers opted for a low-key prayerwalk
along the Weald Way from Gravesend on the River Thames
to Eastbourne on the south coast. By walking together they
maintained their relationships and had a further opportunity
to consider a 1992 European walk.

But plans were already being confirmed. In January 1991, we were passed a document compiled by Christians in Germany outlining a brief history and spiritual background of Berlin and Brandenburg.

The so-called Berlin Declaration was one particular source of concern. On the 15th September 1909 there was a meeting of fifty-six Protestant leaders, mainly from the Evangelical Alliance and from the Association of Pietist Communities. They declared that the Pentecostal movement was 'from below'. None of the accused group was heard. But, as a result of the declaration, Pentecostalism and charismatic renewal has been totally suppressed in Germany. The declaration was reinforced in 1934, 1945, 1956, 1972, 1975 and 1986 and was not publicly repudiated until the 7th November 1991 when some evangelical leaders in Germany began to take some steps to renounce the declaration.

One of our aims in prayerwalking from London to Berlin became that the spiritual impact of this declaration would be reversed and its hold over the spiritual life of Europe broken. As marchers and prayerwalkers gathered in Berlin on the 23rd May 1992, Walter Heidenreich, one of the German March for Jesus team, led them in repentance for the Berlin declaration. In the silence which followed a great wind suddenly blew through the area. We pray that the wind of God's Holy Spirit will blow in increasing measure through the German church and through the whole of Europe.

The Berlin event was the climax of the London to Berlin Prayerwalk which took place from the 23rd April 1992 to 23rd May 1992, and aimed, first and foremost, to be a prayer, praise and witness march involving Christians from all cultures and races who had a vision for a major revival of Christianity in the UK and Europe. There was a great sense of unity in the international prayerwalking team which included old and young; black and white; men and women, from Britain, France, Belgium, Holland, Germany and the USA. Two of the oldest walkers were veterans of World War Two in their seventies.

By prayerwalking we wanted to declare God's concern for what Floyd McClung had dubbed the 'prodigal continent', creating a platform for reconciliation between nations. Prayerwalkers covered approximately 800 miles from London via the Channel to France, Belgium, Holland and Germany, symbolising our desire to see Christ proclaimed across Europe and a sovereign move of the Holy Spirit.

Secondly, the walk was designed to be a prayer focus mobilising the extensive interest in prayer and revival which exists across the continent. This prayer focus culminated on the 23rd May 1992, the first International Day of March for Jesus, when marches took place in most European capitals and many other major cities around the world.

The map of Europe was divided up into thirty-mile bands so that every band was prayed for as the prayerwalkers marched through Europe. A prayer diary focused on key issues, especially asking God for spiritual awakening in Europe. As we passed through each thirty-mile region, we looked for local Christians to join us in concerted prayer for that area.

Thirdly, it was a unique and historic opportunity to express positively the unity and solidarity of God's people, regardless of denomination, race and other divides.

After being welcomed in Calais, a celebration service was an opportunity for us to repent of the insularity of the UK church, and to declare our oneness in Christ with our European brothers and sisters. It was a clear demonstration to principalities and powers of the greatness of God and the lordship of Christ expressed in our lives, with the aim of recovering more ground for God in Europe.

Reconciliation was a key theme as prayerwalkers travelled through Europe. They slept in 1,000 homes en route and received a wonderful welcome in many of the towns they passed through. Often as many as 400 people came out to welcome the walkers. There were tears as well as laughter. In the Dutch town of Margraten they were met by a prayerwalking team and, together with much weeping, they broke bread in the war cemetery.

In East Germany the walkers felt that division was deeply ingrained in the psychology of the people; many longed to feel again the 'fathering' of communism. Graham's song 'Father me' touched many people.

When walkers reached Hamm some stayed in the home of a charismatic Roman Catholic who had been an aircraft gunner defending a dam during the war. He revisited the dam with some of the prayerwalkers and prayed particularly with one of the team who had been involved in bombing Germany. Their growing friendship demonstrated how the prayerwalk focused on reconciliation and rebuilding in contrast to the alienation and destruction of the war.

This new international dimension of the March is thrilling and challenging. Graham says, 'As I was prayerwalking through North Wales, we passed an old power station. It stood like a monument to the megawatts of its most glorious past.

'The church in Europe has become such a monument to a more glorious past. Its missionaries gave their sweat and blood to reach the ends of the earth with the gospel, but now it stands in need of revival.

'One of the most enduring images I carry from the coast-to-coast walks in the UK is that of the great networks of pylons and power lines that crisscross the land. The electricity grid through Britain became a symbol of the prayerwalk team's prayers for networks and relationships to grow among Christians. These would become a spiritual grid system through which the Holy Spirit might flow to flood the nation with the light of the gospel. Churches uniting in prayer would spread this revival power, like the pylons and high tension wires, carrying power throughout the land.

'And now, together with other nations of Europe and beyond, we are plugging into a much greater gospel power grid. This one could stretch across the globe with the pylon and power cables of united prayer, praise and proclamation.'

10

Dynamic Growth

The momentum of March for Jesus Where You Live in 1990 carried us into 1991 as we responded to marchers' requests to repeat the event. For the first time March for Jesus used a complete tailor-made collection of praise and worship songs written by Graham. *Crown Him* focused once again on the personal work of Christ, especially his ascension to the Father's side after his death and resurrection. This album brought together many of the themes drawn from Graham's intercession and meditation on the Torch March and Prayer March Across the Nation and captured the growing international dimension of March for Jesus.

Already marches were taking place in other parts of the world. *Crown Him* put into words and music the song in our hearts:

From the sun's rising unto the sun's setting
Jesus our Lord shall be great in the earth,
And all earth's kingdoms shall be his dominion,
All of creation shall sing of his worth.

Chorus
Let every heart, every voice, every tongue
Join with spirits ablaze.
One in his love we will circle the world
With the song of his praise.
O let all his people rejoice,
And let all the earth hear his voice.

To every tongue, tribe and nation he sends us
To make disciples, to teach, and baptise,
For all authority to him is given
Now as his witnesses we shall arise.

Come let us join with the church from all nations
Cross every border, throw wide every door,
Workers with him as he gathers his harvest
Till earth's far corners our Saviour adore.

The unity which has undergirded our relationships in March for Jesus also found expression in one of the songs based on Psalm 133, entitled 'Join Our Hearts'. But the main focus of *Crown Him* was on crowning Jesus as King, welcoming in his coming kingdom and proclaiming his rule of justice and peace.

March for Jesus took Crown Him out onto the streets for the first time on Saturday, 14th September 1991, and was subtitled 'A Day to Proclaim the King'. More than 300 marches registered with us, though we heard of as many again which took place without registering; we had given the vision away and Christians were fleshing it out in their own ways in their own areas. The impact can only be imagined.

Graham says, 'As the march concept has grown I have developed a list of eight different dynamics which come into effect when we give extravagant praise to our Lord Jesus Christ on the streets. The first is *visibility*. The church in the western world has become something of an anachronism and people have very strange caricatures of the church, largely formed by their own limited experience of it from weddings, christenings and funerals—plus what they see in ceremonies and services on television. I think many people have very little idea of what goes on in churches. So, to take the walls off the church and take the church onto the streets, helps reintroduce the church to the world in its supreme role, that of giving glory and honour to its Lord and Saviour.

'*Public witness* grows out of that as a second dynamic. A crowd of people who are specifically there for Jesus reminds local people that the church is a significant force. Many people have the impression that the church is more or less dead, then suddenly down the street come several thousand people of all ages who are Christians. It really blows away the idea of a dead church and demonstrates the fact that Christ is alive in his church. The name of Jesus is being lifted up. There are banners to read and songs to listen to. If people get caught up in any of the open air prayer meetings or assemblies they know that something real is happening. It is a public witness, a testimony. In one sense whatever people are doing, praying, singing, or just smiling, they are testifying that Jesus Christ is alive and has done something in their lives.

'The third element is *prayer*. I think praise, worship and prayer all overlap each other. You can't say that because you are singing a song you've stopped praying. Particularly if the song is a prayer like "Shine, Jesus Shine". It must be powerful if hundreds or thousands of Christians are praying simultaneous, targeted prayers. We've always tried to direct people's prayers towards what we feel is the God-given purpose of a particular march. It's certainly not vague prayer potshots. It is much more guided. Those of us who have responsibility for the programme always look for the direction and emphasis that we feel God has given us to help focus people's prayers.

'Fourthly there is the *proclamation* of the truth. This is an area on which views differ. But I personally have come to believe that the proclamation of truth, when it is done with faith in the hearts of the proclaimers, does have a spiritual effect. Jesus said, "The words I have spoken to you are spirit and they are life" (John 6:63). It is not just information, there is spiritual power released on our proclamation. I don't think anyone would dispute that in the case of a preacher, preaching the gospel, the Spirit of God rides in on the words. One of the reasons I wrote songs for praise marches in the first place is that I have a conviction

that the power of God is released through the proclamation
of the truth. So part of my vision has been to get the whole
church out on the streets proclaiming the truth.

'The song "We Believe" was a pivotal point in the first
Make Way Carnival of Praise and was used in the March
for Jesus script in 1989 and most others since. I wrote it in
one of those moments when a seed idea turns into a song.
I ended up looking up the Apostles' Creed without really
intending to. Then, with a few adaptations, I put it to music.
People who have used that first Make Way march have said:
"We sensed the power of God when we started to sing 'We
Believe'." Again it is a proclamation of truth which God
himself endorses by his Spirit.

'*Confession of sin* and *intercession* are also important
factors. That is why, on most occasions, I've built these
elements into the music of marches. The prayer "Lord Have
Mercy" is humbly calling upon God, standing in the gap for
those who cannot or will not pray for themselves, inviting
God to send his Spirit and "save the people".

'The sixth dynamic I have identified is *unity*. This was the
area of greatest surprise to me. When I wrote the first Make
Way songs I had no idea how widely they would be used.
Although Ichthus and one or two other isolated groups were
doing some improvised praise on the streets, I thought that
the whole thing was more likely to be taken up by the radical
fringe, if at all. But as soon as we started getting reports
back in the second half of 1986 and throughout 1987, time
and time again local march organisers were saying they
enjoyed a tremendous level of unity between churches. They
were surprised by how many churches had wanted to join
in. It was a tremendous surprise to me that the churches
who were joining in so enthusiastically were by no means
the radical fringe. Fairly conservative churches seemed to
be catching on. Churches across the range of denominations
were actually working together.

'March for Jesus has become a focus for unity. Part of
the reason for that is that it does focus on Jesus, the highest
common denominator, rather than the lowest common

denominator of trying to check our theology and church practices against one another to see what is left on which we can agree. We are starting from what we already agree on—that we love Jesus, that we want to worship him and want his kingdom to come and his will to be done. The content of the marches is credal, again focusing on the highest common denominator; the very core of truth which does unite us. That has been a very important feature on a local level and increasingly on an international level as churches are coming together.

'One of the things that has excited me is the way that a united march down a main street looks like a demonstration but sounds like a carnival. If bystanders take the trouble to read the banners they will see So-and-So Pentecostal Church, then St Someone-else's Anglican Church and Such-and-such Baptist Church, and a Christian fellowship, and so it goes on. The message that comes across is that this is the church in this town, or a substantial part of it. It is not just some fringe group of crazies; they are all out there. The average non-church person usually thinks that Christians are divided; March for Jesus goes a long way to refuting this.

'I believe that God will bring far more unity through churches who learn to worship together than through those who try to nit-pick on theology. March for Jesus celebrates the unity that we already have as a gift from God—won through what Jesus did on the cross.

'The seventh aspect of March for Jesus is a baptism of *boldness*. The church in this country cannot claim adequately to have done its job of proclaiming the faith. There is a spell of silence that cripples many churches. There is a fear of what people might think and an insecurity: "If I'm to share my faith what do I say?" Ordinary Christians are often quite intimidated by the idea of publicly sharing their faith. The popular concept is that you have to stand up on a soapbox and shout your testimony on a street corner, or you have to accost somebody on the street and share your faith. Each of those things can be valid, but I think that one of the special things about praise marches is that they enable all believers, of whatever age, to testify publicly to their faith. Obviously it is less costly if you are in a big crowd, but it is certainly a significant step towards being bolder in testimony.

'On several occasions when I have been involved in a pre-march assembly I have picked up a sense of nervousness among people who haven't done it before. It is a new situation and they feel a bit exposed. They are out of their usual context and are not really sure they want to be there. If they start going through the main street they think of all the people they know, like their neighbours who might be out shopping and will spot them on the march and want an explanation later. But about half way through the march a distinct change of mood comes across the crowd. Suddenly they don't care any more what people think of them. They've got so excited in their own spirits. Something has been released. The spell of silence has been broken. A new boldness has come on them, and by the time they finish they want to go round again.

'I think that's a spiritual dynamic. I know the principle is there in Scripture: "If you confess with your mouth . . ." (Romans 10:9). An open confession of faith strengthens and confirms the whole process of salvation. I think people in many churches are being released into a new boldness. Individual churches hold themselves in low esteem, but when several gather together and the police have to stop the traffic for them, and churches discover that they are the biggest march or public event ever to have happened in their town in living memory, they suddenly wake up and say, "We're a significant force!"'

'Finally, March for Jesus is a springboard for evangelism. I say springboard because in itself, March for Jesus is designed not to be an evangelistic event but to be a witness event. Someone standing in the streets who sees a friend go past might catch a few snippets of the songs or read a few banners, but they are not going to get an in-depth understanding of the gospel.

'I believe that it is time for Christians from different

backgrounds, traditions and nations to come together in a massive show of love for Jesus. The world needs to see the glory of God displayed in the lives of ordinary people. The church needs to break out of its buildings, to let the light of Christ shine brightly in the darkness.

'March for Jesus takes the walls off the church in a fresh expression of worship which is uniting Christians in joyful processions and open-air celebrations of praise, prayer and proclamation throughout the world.'

This fresh inspiration has prompted many new ideas. One of the initiatives to be launched from the March for Jesus springboard has been Challenge 2000. Lynn Green explains: 'As larger and larger crowds gathered for marches, we realised that there was a force of at least a quarter of a million Christians in Britain who were agreed that every person in the country should hear the gospel. For months we asked, "How would God want us to go about this great task? Should we plan to march in every street in the country? Do we aim to communicate the gospel repeatedly by different means, like door to door, through literature or evangelistic preaching campaigns?"

'We didn't think for a moment that we were in the position to control the efforts of all these Christians, but we knew we could have some positive influence on them.

'Finally Roger and I were at a conference where someone spoke about Discipling A Whole Nation, or DAWN. It was explained that DAWN is not a programme or campaign, but a strategy to mobilise as many churches as possible to place a living, growing, Christ-centred church within easy reach of everyone.

'We saw that this was the answer to our question! What could be more biblical and practical at the same time? We could encourage denominations and networks of churches to keep planting more churches after their own kind. If we could aim to have an active, Christ-centred church for about every 1,000 people in England, then that congregation could and should assume responsibility for the people who live around them. (Peter Brierley in *Christian England* calculated that in 1989 there were 1,200 people in England for every church [p 62] but the average church has only 200–300 seats—and that says nothing about whether the churches are "active and Christ-centred" or not.)

'We could see many clear advantages to this kind of strategy. If there was an active congregation of believers in every village and every neighbourhood of our cities and towns, then the gospel could be put before the people on a regular and ongoing basis. That would be consistent with God's demonstrated desire to make the gospel incarnate within every community.

'It would promote church planting, and church growth statistics have shown conclusively that church attendance grows dramatically when a denomination or group of churches concentrates on planting new churches.

'It would promote unity and co-operation between the various denominations and networks of churches while still respecting their distinctives. The DAWN strategy would encourage Methodist churches to plant and revitalise Methodist churches, Baptist churches to concentrate on more Baptist churches etc. Unity would be promoted as the various denominations and networks meet together to co-ordinate their efforts and avoid duplication where possible.

'Each denomination or group would be encouraged to continue developing its own evangelistic strategy and its own model of church life; however, a national strategy would be seen when all of the individual plans were blended together.

'When we thought about how the church in England could make use of this strategy, we realised God had already prompted some movement in this direction. We were greatly encouraged as we noted some developments. Several denominations had begun to recognise the importance of planting new congregations. Some of them had already started to set goals for how many new congregations they planned to establish in the 1990s. In other denominations, including the Baptists and Anglicans, there were regular church planting conferences which attracted hundreds of leaders. George Carey was the main speaker at an Anglican conference and the Baptists were offering a degree course in church planting! The New Churches have demonstrated a commitment to church planting during the last decade and have accounted for the great majority of church growth for that period.

'Perhaps most importantly, there were many towns and cities where the church leaders were working together in remarkable unity. In these places, a local DAWN strategy would provide a wonderful framework for co-operation and even greater unity. Church leaders in some towns and cities were already working together with this kind of shared strategy.

'Against the background of all this encouragement, a consultation on church planting was held in the spring of 1991. Eighty leaders from more than twenty denominations met at the invitation of March for Jesus, the Evangelical Alliance and the Bible Society, to hear from one another and to plan for the future.

'During the three days we spent together, we enjoyed good unity and fellowship and were encouraged by reports from the many groups which were represented. Some of them could report that they had recently developed quite comprehensive plans for growth during this Decade of Evangelism. Others confessed that they were still in the days of small beginnings, but a spirit of hope permeated every part of the consultation.

'The members of the consultation agreed that further steps towards a national plan for growth should be taken. They gave a mandate to a representative group of leaders who would continue to meet and plan towards a much larger conference in 1992. March for Jesus continued to serve the vision by providing the financial and legal framework for the group and the congress, which was called Challenge 2000.'

The event was devised under the March for Jesus banner, but soon took on a separate life of its own. The congress brought together over 700 church leaders from thirty-two denominations and new church affiliations who, by the end of the time together, had set a faith goal: 'Twenty per cent of the population attending church by the end of the twentieth century by planting 20,000 new churches.'

Lynn Green sums up the challenge: 'Can the body of Christ reverse its decline and once again play a vital role in the life of this nation? Can the Great Commission be completed? Yes, it can—and the best way to go about it is to aim to plant a living, growing, Christ-centred congregation within easy reach of everyone.'

II

Going Global

As March for Jesus has caught the imagination of Christians throughout the United Kingdom, so news has spread worldwide. The enthusiasm of other countries for March for Jesus has amazed us. In 1990 we began receiving reports of marches in the USA and South Africa. We tentatively suggested a 1992 Europe-wide march to contacts in other European capitals and invited them to observe marches in the UK. Their response was overwhelmingly positive.

When we first dreamed of marches throughout Europe, the Berlin Wall was still standing and half the continent was governed by communist regimes. On the 23rd May 1992, when more than 250,000 European marchers took to the streets in Moscow, Gdansk, Warsaw, Prague, Budapest, Bucharest and Tirana, as well as Western European capitals, March for Jesus–Europe became a reality.

Reconciliation and unity were key themes in the forty-seven European marches. Christians in the Cypriot capital of Nicosia marched to the green line dividing Greek and Turkish Cyprus and prayed for reconciliation. In the Polish city of Gdansk, Protestants and Roman Catholics joined in equal numbers to march together through the city—the first ever Polish sign of unity between the two groups.

About 6,000 marchers took to the streets of Prague on the day—both Czechs and Slovaks—and their script included prayers for their General Election. Organisers said, 'We do not remember a joint activity of such a broad spectrum of churches. We are looking forward to the march next year.'

In Berlin 60,000 Christians marched for Jesus along Unter den Linden and through the Brandenburg gate; the same route that Hitler used to parade the might and power of the Third Reich. Most of the Christian denominations were represented in a joyful and colourful celebration which was an impressive sign of the changes taking place in Germany. In Vienna, Protestant and Catholic leaders prayed together about divisions in the church. The Mayor of Vienna commented, 'I believe in the power of faith. It's exactly the power that is missing in today's world.'

Turkish Christians were not allowed to march, so they held a 'Sail for Jesus'! In Istanbul about 100 adults plus children hired a boat and sailed up the Bosporus which divides Europe from Asia. They stopped on the Asian side near some mosques to pray, then sailed back to the European side for a time of worship.

A boat was also brought into use by March for Jesus in Malta. They marched along the coast with the MV Redeemer sailing alongside decked out with banners and flags. As marchers continued in praise and prayer on land, the MV Redeemer sailed on to St Paul's Bay where the Apostle Paul is said to have been shipwrecked.

Christians in Tirana, Albania, were particularly glad to be able to take part in an international event. The Tirana march started in the city's main park on the plinth where the statue of Stalin used to be. By the time the 300 marchers reached Tirana's main square numbers had swelled to between 2,000 and 3,000.

Lynne Quanrud, one of the marchers in Albania, said, 'There were three main evangelical fellowships on the organising committee, but on the day we had representatives from other fellowships in Tirana and the rest of Albania, as well as people from the Catholic and Orthodox churches. It was a very special time, particularly when we sang "Shine, Jesus, Shine" in the four directions of the compass. There was a real sense of blessing on our country as we did this.

'It has been the talk of the town. One of the most encouraging aspects was to see how local believers really entered into it. They were involved in writing the programme, translating songs, making banners, decorating the truck, distributing flags and balloons. There was no sense of it being something imposed on them by foreigners.'

Christians in Moscow also took part and were glad to be involved in an initiative which allowed them to be Russians rather than Western teaching-fodder. The Moscow marchers —500 in all—left the rallying point two miles from the Kremlin led by dancers in Russian costumes. Dougie Brown, a worship leader from the UK who was in the city for the event, said, 'Seeing hundreds of Spirit-filled Russian Christians freely glorifying God on the street was almost too much. I was seeing with my eyes what I had seen in my heart for twenty-four years. I couldn't believe I was seeing it.'

Even in war-torn Yugoslavia fifty people gathered to pray in Belgrade and were planning to bring Evangelicals, Catholics and Orthodox church members together for a march at a later date.

Marchers throughout Europe signed statements to their governments. The UK statement highlighted the 'door of opportunity' which the Single European Act presents and called on heads of government to

> exercise your authority on behalf of the weak and work for European unity in the name of justice. Righteousness exalts a nation, and the future of Europe demands that those entrusted with the responsibility of governing should themselves acknowledge the rule of Jesus Christ and apply biblical principles in governing nations.

The statement ended with a commitment to pray for the government.

Across the Atlantic American Christians also took to the streets. In 143 cities they marched for Jesus, on the same day as their European brothers and sisters. Tom Pelton, USA National Co-ordinator, said, 'With the release of the *Crown Him* music in the USA the idea of taking praise onto

the streets really caught fire. It's very exciting to see the
speed at which things are happening.' When Gerald was
invited to appear on the American TV shows *Heart to Heart*,
and CBN's *700 Club* with Sheila Walsh, interest in March
for Jesus spread even more rapidly.

In the wake of the Los Angeles riots which had spread
throughout the States in the month before the marches, reconciliation was a significant theme. In Memphis, Tennessee,
a particularly segregated city, a white pastor and a black
pastor worked together to organise the day. They were
refused permission to march on the route taken by Martin
Luther King Jr. Instead they opted for a site where blacks
were auctioned as slaves a hundred years ago. Rain started
to fall as the marchers—50:50 black and white—set off. So
they stopped and prayed together. The rain then stopped
until they had finished marching.

In Cleveland, Tennessee, healing between races was
reported as a result of their march. In the border town of
El Paso, Mexico, permission was given for Mexicans to join
the march singing and praying in both Spanish and English.

A black pastor organised the Newport, Virginia, march
and was amazed to find marchers equally balanced racially.
The Catholic priest from the largest Catholic church in the
city was so excited about the event he said he would like to
see his whole parish take part next year.

There was repentance for the 1906 lynching of three black
men in the public square where the Springfield, Missouri,
prayer assembly was held, before 3,000 Christians set off to
March for Jesus—another demonstration of the reconcilia-
tions which marked the day.

Commitment to local communities was another hallmark
of the American marches. An offering at the march in
Austin, Texas, raised $20,000 for the city's Children's
Hospital. In St Louis, Missouri, marchers took up an
offering to pay for a scheme to employ inner-city youngsters.
Marchers in Columbia, Missouri, cleaned up a city park
after the march, removing rubbish and broken glass as well
as cleaning the toilets.

The event attracted a great deal of attention in states
across the continent. The Governor of the State of Iowa
marched in Des Moine, Iowa, because he wanted to set a
precedent for the other forty-nine governors across America.
In Jackson, Tennessee, the Mayor of the city marched and
issued a proclamation officially declaring the 23rd May
1992 as March for Jesus Day. Chart-topping singer
Amy Grant marched with 15,000 Christians in Nashville,
Tennessee, and Christians in the military town of Killeen,
Texas, overcame the fact that their march clashed with a
parade by joining the scheduled event with a March for
Jesus float. As they passed the review stand the general,
who was taking the salute, stood to his feet and lifted his
hands for Jesus!

At the end of the day, when over half a million Christians
in 200 cities across Europe and North America had marched
for Jesus, Gerald Coates said, 'March for Jesus has built up
over the years a growing awareness that we are about more
than singing and unity. We are affecting the social fabric of
our nation.'

Requests for march information have also come from
Christians in Singapore, Canada, Japan, South Africa,
Korea and New Zealand—a global interest which has led
to plans for marches around the world on the same day in
1994. This 'Day to Change the World' began almost as a
joke; a pipe-dream we bandied about as we were drafting
this book, until Peter Wagner of the Church Growth
movement was ministering at the Ichthus Christian Fellowship. He had a meal with Roger and Gerald and was excited
by the March for Jesus concept. His enthusiasm put the
global dream into sharp focus and he suggested a worldwide March for Jesus on the 25th June 1994 coinciding with
the AD 2000 World Evangelisation conference in Seoul,
Korea.

He anticipates up to two million Christians will be on the
streets marching for Jesus in Seoul on that day. The event
will be preceded by forty days of prayer and fasting. The
day before, Christians will be invited to spend the night in

prayer asking God to pour out his blessing on the world. When 25th June arrives Christians will be invited to march in every capital city in the world as 2pm comes round in each time zone.

As we give our full support to this global initiative, we can only say it is in God's hands. He has given us a vision; we have offered it back to him and will continue to give it away to all who want to join us in proclaiming Christ as Lord of all the earth.

Marching for Jesus is not new. It is part of the great tradition of prophetic symbolism. It shows that the church is a pilgrim church and is in this world to go places—it has a purpose and we are symbolising that as we march.

It also symbolises the fact that life is transient: we are not here for ever; we start at the beginning, finish at the end and are all just passing through—aliens and strangers. And it is right that it is in public: not to draw attention to ourselves like the Pharisees who paraded themselves on street corners in order to be seen by people, but to point towards God and to show that the church is a people of prayer. We are a people in whom God is present. The Holy Spirit moves with us, and his presence with us can be seen by people outside.

Marching for Jesus is a prophetic action which demonstrates that 'the meek shall inherit the earth'. Each footstep on the march is an action which claims the ground and says, 'This is God's world. We are claiming it for God.' There is a fighting spirit as when Jesus rode into Jerusalem on an ass with a whole crowd after him shouting 'Hosanna!', and when Joshua took the land of Canaan—but our aggression is against spiritual powers, not against human beings. Our marching says that we do not inherit the earth by buying it, nor by inheriting it from people, but by shifting the spiritual powers that have been allocated in the structures of nations and the strongholds of human solidarities. By marching we say to principalities and powers: 'This is not your ground—it is God's ground. God's will is going to be done on earth as it is in heaven.'

Marching for Jesus also shows the world that Christianity is a people's movement and it belongs to the grassroots, not to a hierarchy of power. Christianity is for ordinary people; it is especially for the poor. We don't believe that a 'respectable' church will ever re-evangelise Britain or any other nation. There is a degree of unrespectability to marching down the street, but it's that kind of church which is going to get the job done. It's the sort of thing that ordinary people are doing every day of their lives, whether they are selling from their barrows or out shopping. Ordinary people are always on the streets; it's only the rich who get into Rolls Royces and don't bother to go to the supermarket.

Marching for Jesus also demonstrates that the church is people not buildings. Most people think the church is a building—they're taught that way. March for Jesus is one day in the year when the walls and roof come off those buildings; the world sees the church in its own area, and Christians discover that the church is bigger than any one congregation. Together we can encourage and help each other.

By marching together and not as individual congregations we demonstrate the unity we have in Christ; a unity achieved at the 'highest common denominator' of the cross. In the local marches the impact on the national media may have been weak at first, but the impact on the lives of the marchers, their churches and their communities has been huge, whether there were twenty or two thousand marchers. When Baptists, Methodists, Anglicans, Catholics, Brethren, New Churches, Salvationists and others march through their town or city centre together, it makes a strong statement about our God.

Finally, marching shows that we're *for* something. The happiness, the enjoyment, the balloons, the bright colours, the singing, the fancy dress, all contribute to an atmosphere of carnival and celebration which prophetically asserts the positive nature of living God's way in God's world.

In the past, when Anglicans first beat the bounds of their parishes, or people went on pilgrimages, there was always an air of festivity. These events took place on holy days which became our holidays. People did them to express their life together. They wanted to stand for goodness and truth and push the enemy out. These things are all expressed in symbolism, but we believe that there is more to prophetic symbolism than simply putting over concepts. We think that there is actually a release of power through symbolism.

The object of the first March for Jesus in 1987 was to make a bold proclamation of Christ in areas which have significance as seats of power in Britain. We trust that marching for Jesus helps bring a greater visibility to God in his people. It introduces some believers to spiritual warfare, and others to the benefits of practical unity.

When we march for Jesus we are not rambling for pleasure, we are wrestling to bring about real changes in the heavenlies. And all this shall be done in union with our Christ 'who always leads us forth in triumph' (2 Corinthians 2:14).

> I looked, and there before me was a white cloud, and seated on the cloud was one 'like a son of man' with a crown of gold on his head and a sharp sickle in his hand. Then another angel came out of the temple and called in a loud voice to him who was sitting on the cloud, 'Take your sickle and reap, because the time to reap has come, for the harvest of the earth is ripe.' So he who was seated on the cloud swung his sickle over the earth, and the earth was harvested (Revelation 14:14–16, NIV).

APPENDIX
March for Jesus Theology

This final chapter is adapted from a talk given by Roger Forster at the March for Jesus European Consultation in October 1990. It repeats some of the points in the main text, but provides a useful summary of the theological basis of March for Jesus.

March for Jesus is an event which has captured the minds of many people in nations all over the world. In the UK alone over 200,000 people have taken to the streets on one single day. In 1992 Christians in many European capitals participated in marches, joined by many across the USA. In 1994, in identification with the congress for world evangelisation taking place in Korea, it is expected that marches in each time band will ring the earth with prayer.

In essence March for Jesus:

(a) takes the walls off our church buildings and shows what the church really is—people enjoying God's love in Jesus;

(b) asserts that the earth is the Lord's (Psalm 24) and claims the territory for God by prayer;

(c) takes praise and prayer expressing love for Jesus onto the streets, thus witnessing to heaven and earth of a lifestyle of worship.

Some people, however, have been a little less enthusiastic. Others, being ill-informed concerning our vision and, we

believe, our obedience to God, have been openly critical.
I want therefore to give seven reasons for marching, in order
both to outline our underlying theology and to answer some
of the criticisms levelled against us.

(1) Obedience

The need for obedience to God seems obvious but it's very
important. In the final analysis I must be able to say with
confidence, 'God told us to march.' I am convinced that
God spoke to us and told us to march. Our understanding
of the theology of what we were doing came later after we
had begun to act in obedience to what we believed the Holy
Spirit was asking us to do.

Let me give an illustration. Many times in the Bible God
gave the prophets specific instructions about things they
were to do without revealing to them the reasons for their
actions. Jeremiah, for example, was told to take his waist
band (or loin-cloth—his under-clothes we'd say today) and
bury it in a certain place. That was a bizarre thing to do
and if any of us were to do that today we'd certainly have
some ecclesiastical authorities breathing down our necks
demanding an explanation! If we then responded by saying,
'I don't know why God told me to bury my underwear under
a rock out there in the desert,' they would probably conclude
that we were crazy and bringing the testimony of Jesus into
disrepute.

However, when God spoke to Jeremiah a second time
and he retrieved his waist band, he then interpreted his
action as an illustration of what happens when a nation is
cast off by God and left desolate. God explained that he
had cast Israel off and that spiritual decay had now set in.
Jeremiah's prophetic act of burying his waist band made
sense to the people. It was understood and remembered
(Jeremiah 13:1–11).

God may tell us to do something that we do not fully
understand at the moment. Why does God work like this?

Because revelation must be involved with if not preceded by obedience. It is as we obey God that we engage with and enter into the truth of his word. We do not adequately understand the Scriptures until we are prepared to do them (John 7:17). It is the Holy Spirit who leads us into all truth (John 16:13) and the theology of marching will emerge as we engage in it and listen to what the Spirit is saying.

Some put forward the objection that there is 'no marching in the Gospels, Acts or New Testament letters'. Even if this were true, it would in no way invalidate marching for Jesus if it was initiated by the Spirit of God. I emphasise this point because it seems that people use the 'biblical precedent' argument to justify inactivity, non-participation and criticism. You cannot say that, because there is no explicit biblical precedent for marching, the Holy Spirit will never tell us to do it. In fact, it can be dangerous to take such a stance because it kills (John 5:39ff, 7:52, 8:5ff, 19:7; 2 Corinthians 3:6). The Spirit of God is constantly revealing to his people creative and dynamic ways of engaging the powers and advancing the kingdom in the particular culture and context in which we now live. Of course it goes without saying that true guidance will never contradict the Scriptures.

Since we started marching, we have understood year by year more of what is happening supernaturally as we have sought to obey God. We didn't have a clearly defined theology of marching when we first began, but it is becoming clearer as we examine the Scriptures and discover the rich models that it contains, and increasingly see the power and effect of our actions in society.

Let me relate a little of our history in marching. Before the first national March for Jesus we at the Ichthus Christian Fellowship had often held local marches. I remember two particular occasions when we marched through Soho, London's red-light district. I began to pray that Soho would become the cleanest place in London, that the power of the Holy Spirit would chase out every unclean spirit and cleanse the district. Just a short time later Westminster Police raided the whole area of Soho—I have never heard of such an operation before or since—and every illegal sex show was shut down (the legal ones, of course, unfortunately continue to operate for the present). People say to us: 'Do you really think that was anything to do with marching for Jesus?' Yes! We can't march through areas like that, call on the name of Jesus and ask God to intervene without something happening, can we? Or don't we believe in prayer?

Of course marching isn't anything new; after all, people in the Christian church have been marching for 2,000 years. Every Christian festival, despite the gradual addition of pagan elements over the years, was built on Old Testament models of holy days when God's people would come out and enjoy his presence and one another's company. Our Christian festivals parallel the tribes of Israel going up to Jerusalem three times a year to enjoy the presence of God. In the English parish system the priest led his congregation around the boundaries of the parish every year and 'beat the bounds'. The aim was to shift the spiritual powers of the parish. That was part of the priest's ministry.

The Salvation Army with its militant drum banging and its bugle blowing marched in a very virile way, and from the inner-city slums of London was born a movement which today is worldwide. In marching for Jesus we are following precedents that have existed throughout the history of the Christian church.

There is nothing new in what we are doing.

Is it in the Bible?

Before I move on, let me give a brief view of the various criticisms levelled at us by other Christians after the UK marches.

Our critics viewed what we were doing back in 1987 as another odd abberation on the evangelical scene, saying that we had virtually no grounds for marching for Jesus because it had no precedent in the New Testament. The objection to our practice went something like this: any marching in the Bible was in the Old Testament; since there were no marches in the New Testament there is no ground for talking about Joshua and the walls of Jericho, or Nehemiah and the walls of Jerusalem in the same breath as the Houses of Parliament and other contemporary institutions.

You will remember, however, that Jesus very clearly said that he had not come to destroy the law and the prophets, but to fulfil them—to fill them full with himself, to fill them out. Consequently, there is nothing that can be dismissed in the Old Testament since all of it is to be seen in the light of the completed revelation in Christ.

We seek to understand the Bible through the eyes of Jesus. That doesn't sound particularly extreme, does it? However, conservative, evangelical theology over the past 100 years has been dominated by the historical critical method which seeks only to understand what the Scriptures meant to the original writer and his original audience, nothing more. In contrast, throughout church history Christians have tried to grasp how Jesus understood the Old Testament and how he is seen in all the Scriptures. Surely, therefore, there is relevance in the Old Testament models and pictures to justify our marching for Jesus if there is a proper exegesis of these models through the light of Christ himself? Remember that the New Testament church had only the Old Testament as its Scripture (plus one or two letters) and the oral tradition of *kerygma*. They found relevance in the Old Testament models. We simply seek to follow in their footsteps.

Out of touch with real issues?

The criticisms raised in 1988 were different from the previous year. We had tried hard to involve the minority communities in our nation, Blacks, Asians and others in the march, to show that we are all one in Christ. However, at that point we had not yet seen a great response from these communities. To our astonishment a critic went into print with the objection that we were not interested in social action, in kingdom issues concerning race and the poor, and the problems of public life. Now, of course, those who knew us realised that this was far from the truth. We at Ichthus have Black and White co-equally leading the people of God and our critic might have remembered that when we use the word 'nation' it includes all the minorities that exist within an actual political entity, but he criticised us for using such terms in our songs, and we were told that praying for the nation was racist.

Of course, we could only answer by our own example and tried to say, 'Even if you don't agree with what we are doing, surely you can applaud the Lord who leads us in different pathways. Come and see what we are doing in social action in our cities.' Pioneer, YWAM and Ichthus who are the three convening bodies of March for Jesus, each have a vast amount of social and political action going on. Just because on one day in the year we also happen to be marching doesn't mean to say that on the other 364 days we are not working as servants of God in society with compassion and mercy.

Making trouble?

After the 1989 march the only criticism we received was that we caused a lot of trouble! Now I guess that Jesus also caused a lot of trouble—as did the prophets of God, and the church throughout history. We certainly ought to be stirring things up because there's a lot of sin and unrighteousness around. If we do nothing, evil will rule the day.

We caused terrific trouble in our own area because we were one of the few churches who were willing to make a noise about the advancement of homosexual activity via political legislation through schools and education. Not many people stood with us, but I knew that personally I would not be able to stand before God in the last day if I was not willing to be counted at that time. For all the criticism it brought upon us, I knew it was something we had to do.

When we have marches we do cause trouble. We hold up traffic, we make some people a little late for their work and disrupt their shopping trips. Sometimes we make a bit of a

noise and some people shut their windows, but most open
them to listen or catch the sweets or balloons we might
distribute. We could have reminded our critics that there
was colossal 'trouble' every night in London when Billy
Graham was preaching. Traffic jams abounded and public
transport was disrupted in the areas where his crusades were
held. However, nobody raised their voice then, presumably
because it was more 'acceptable'. Marching, however, was
a 'new' thing so it was thought fair game to criticise it. We
took courage from Elijah, 'the troubler' (1 Kings 18:17).

Shaky theology?

After the march in 1990 we experienced a more serious
criticism. One or two Anglican churchmen said that our
theology concerning principalities and powers was unaccept-
able, unbiblical and dangerous. Consequently, they were
encouraging the established church to withdraw from March
for Jesus.

Theological study during the last twenty years has been
very exercised to try and understand principalities and
powers in greater depth. Professor G.B. Caird of Oxford
University was early on the scene. Oscar Cullmann, a very
incisive biblical scholar, has also enquired into the nature
of principalities and powers. Walter Wink, from a mildly
liberal standpoint, has undertaken a very extensive enquiry
into demonology, spiritual forces and the angels of churches
and nations. Each of these theologians would say that,
despite their study and research, they do not yet fully
understand these areas of biblical thought, and let me add
that we don't presume to understand everything about
principalities and powers either.

We don't know how to engage totally the spiritual forces
of darkness that are vested in the structures of society. We
don't know exactly what happens when we declare the
victory of Jesus into the cosmos. What we do know is that
something does happen even when we don't fully understand
it. This is why we feel it is valid to understand March for

Jesus as having an impact upon the spiritual condition of the society in which we live.

An article on principalities and powers in one of the Christian monthly magazines in Britain was also used by our critics against us. The article, which was very clear and concise, had specified three ways in which we might understand the powers.

The first was as the evangelical-social-activist generally sees it. Principalities and powers are perceived to be located in the structures of society; local and national government, economic institutions and education. Thus to encounter the powers involves influencing and changing these structures—something which, of course, most biblical Christians are seeking to do. Let me assure you again, those of us who actually instituted March for Jesus are very much engaged in this activity throughout the year, often feeling overwhelmed by the scale of the problems we confront.

The magazine editor had added a picture that represented his view of the three positions outlined in the article. Beside the text outlining the evangelical-social-activist understanding there was a photograph of a clergyman in his ecclesiastical dress, carrying a cross and leading a CND (Campaign for Nuclear Disarmament) march. Here then is the church marching into action and confronting the principalities and powers.

The second view was that principalities and powers are engaged only when we preach the gospel. The corresponding photograph was of Billy Graham preaching. Here the church is thrusting back the spiritual forces by declaration, preaching and conversion. We also agree that this is crucial and have given our lives to preaching and teaching, calling men, women and children to repentance and faith.

The third view was that principalities and powers are engaged when we pray. Daniel is, of course, a classic example. As he prays the Prince of Persia and the Prince of Greece come under various restrictions or directions. In a similar way we also wrestle with spiritual forces and engage them in warfare (Ephesians 6:12). When you begin to fast

and pray you become aware of the demonic realm. The
picture linked with this view of the powers was a shot of
March for Jesus. I suppose it was this juxtaposition of text
and photo that gave rise to the criticism in which our
confronting principalities and powers was described as a
'corporate exorcism'. As we marched, sang and prayed we
were supposed to be corporately exorcising the Stock
Market, the police force, education and so on.

It may be argued that some institutions need it, but we
didn't actually say that! We do believe, however, that as we
pray and praise and declare in the name of Jesus, mountains
are cast into the sea (Mark 11:23ff). The physical, psycho-
logical and spiritual forces that stand in the way of the
kingdom of God are driven back. March for Jesus holds no
official specific theological understanding nor exclusive
viewpoint. All believers of all viewpoints are welcomed to
share together.

(2) Unity

So we march out of obedience to God. But secondly, we
march because there is unity in marching. Obviously, if you
march in step as an army you soon learn to keep together!
In the same way our unity is expressed by moving together
as Christians from all denominations and backgrounds,
standing together to be counted for the Lord. When Jesus
prayed: 'I pray that they may be one that the world might
believe' (John 17:21) he did not expect to wait two thousand
years for it to happen. It is an insult to the Father (and
would certainly put me off my prayer life) if Jesus had to
wait two thousand years for an answer to prayer. Within
hours of that prayer, 'I pray that they may be one,' Jesus
went to the cross and was crucified so that every difference
and distinction, everything that is a barrier in our relationships, everything that stands in the way of the human race
being reconciled, might be nailed to the cross. Then he rose.
One new man, carrying with him a totally new humanity
that could never be anything but wholly at one with each

other. If we are not one with each other it is because we will not receive the unity of the Spirit which is the gift of God which Paul enjoins us to keep, not make (Ephesians 4:1–3).

It is because we will not stand in that unity that we remain unreconciled. Enough of people with long religious faces making pining noises about how hurtful it is that we are not one—it's time we got out there and accepted that God in Christ has already made us one! It's time that we stood in that unity. It's lovely to get into the streets and stand together for Jesus and demonstrate a love which the world cannot reproduce or copy. It comes directly from God as a gift. Unity is a very, very important part of the kind of evangelism that will actually be demonstrated by marching for Jesus.

(3) Prayer and praise

Thirdly, marching for Jesus is prayer and praise. We take our worship out onto the streets so that we might know God's presence in our midst as he inhabits the praises of his people (Psalm 22:3). As the body of Christ marches, there is an opportunity for God to be manifested in his people, something which the majority of unbelievers would never otherwise see, feel or know because they never come inside our buildings. But as we pray, praise and march together God is in the midst of us, just as he was when they carried the ark in the Old Testament days. God inhabits the praises of his people and we minister God's presence out into society because he is with us as we march. While we remain shut up in our church buildings the world will not see or receive his love. As we move out together and the praises of God resound in the air, then the presence of the Holy Spirit is manifested in our midst and people know the living God is among us.

There was a moment during the 1989 march when Gerald Coates and I knocked at No 10 Downing Street and delivered a letter to the Government. We rejoined the march just as a particular section of marchers was finishing a song. Then everyone began to pray together.

It was awe-inspiring. The spectators on the pavements watched in silence. You could feel the presence of God on the street. Of course, there was plenty of joy, dancing and celebration as well, but at that moment as we prayed together God was in that place and everyone knew it. Probably most onlookers had never seen Christianity like this. Now it was being demonstrated right in front of them on the street. Paul speaks of this corporate evangelistic impact where all convict the unbeliever when he comes into a gathering of God's people. 'But if all prophesy, and an unbeliever or outsider enters, he is convicted by all, he is called to account by all, the secrets of his heart are disclosed; and so falling on his face, he will worship God and declare that God is really among you' (1 Corinthians 14:24–25). Why should we not go out into the streets to see the same result?

At the dedication of the rebuilt walls of Jerusalem Nehemiah organised a march around the walls. He called that march 'Thanksgivings' (Nehemiah 12:31,38). One 'Thanksgivings' went to the left, the other 'Thanksgivings' went to the right and eventually the two came together (most English texts translate the word 'choirs', but the Hebrew word really means 'Thanksgivings'). Every time they put their foot down they were giving thanks with their bodies. This is what we are doing in our day when we go out on the streets. It's a prayer-praise-march, an offering to God, a 'Thanksgiving' going up to him.

(4) Proclamation

Fourthly, marching for Jesus makes a theological statement. In his account of riding into Jerusalem on an ass Matthew quotes two verses of Scripture which interpret our Lord's prophetic action. One says, 'Behold, your King comes to you, meek and lowly, riding upon an ass, the colt, the foal of an ass' (Zechariah 9:9). The other verse is, 'Blessed is

he that comes in the name of the Lord' (Psalm 118:26).
Intriguingly, the psalm from which this verse is taken says,
'The stone which the builders have rejected has become the
head of the corner' (Psalm 118:22). These two scriptures
authenticate who Jesus is and give theological content and
background to his prophetic action of entering Jerusalem
in this way.

Jesus was making a statement that he was the Messiah,
but he had also previously warned the crowd (Luke 13:35)
that they would not truly 'see' him until they bowed the
knee and said, 'Blessed is he who comes in the name of the
Lord.' Psalm 118:22 is a warning that Israel would be blind
and would reject the Messiah ('the stone which the builders
rejected') but if they submitted and said 'Blessed is he that
comes in the name of the Lord' their eyes would be opened
and they would see by revelation who Jesus really is. He
was declaring in a beautiful way the servant nature of his
messiahship by the prophetic act of riding into Jerusalem
on an ass.

When we march we are making a theological statement
and also looking for a response. We are saying that the
church is on the move and we want to be counted and known
publicly as disciples of Jesus. We are saying that Christians
standing together are the real church, not the buildings we
meet in and for which we pay lots of money.

I should add that we had another criticism, which was
later withdrawn when the high-ranking ecclesiastical gentle-
man concerned received first-hand information. He had read
criticism in the secular press from one of his clergy describing
us as Nazis. I suppose that in the twentieth century that
description is one of the most insulting statements one could
make of a fellow-believer or indeed of anyone. However
our critic backed that up further by saying we have had
Lenin, Stalin, Hitler, Saddam Hussein, the IRA—and now
March for Jesus. It was very sad that such statements could
be made, sad that a responsible official could be so
irresponsible. To march for love, truth, humility and justice
is what our Saviour does: 'Gird your sword upon your thigh,

O mighty one, in your glory and majesty. In your majesty ride forth victoriously for the cause of truth and to defend the right; let your right hand teach you dread deeds!' (Psalm 45:3–4).

Most people involved in the secular media love the happiness, warmth, love, acceptance and friendship found on the march. We are soldiers of Jesus Christ. That is what he calls us to be, good soldiers of Christ (2 Timothy 2:3; Numbers 8:24 'war the warfare' in Hebrew). Soldiers and armies march, and as we march we are expecting to evoke a response from bystanders ('Blessed is he who comes in the name of the Lord') who will consequently have their eyes opened to recognise Jesus as the Messiah.

The day after that 1990 March for Jesus, a television programme for children included footage of the event. Soon after the programme, a man phoned up one of our congregations and said: 'Hey, I never knew church was like that, it looks good. Can I come next week?' That was because he had seen the church as it really is. He didn't realise it was like that. He had a wrong model and until we get out on the streets people will continue to have wrong models. What else will they have to look at? Buildings? Great huge doors? Towers? They don't have a clue what's going on inside. How are they going to see the church unless the church comes to them? This is where the church belongs. It was also where Jesus belonged. He spent most of his time on the streets, in the fields, out in the open. He didn't even preach in synagogues very often—and when he did they sometimes threw him out (John 9:22). Occasionally he went to people's homes—but then they pulled the roof off and he was back in the open air again!

Our marching is a theological statement that reflects Jesus' triumphal march into the cross, out of the tomb, leading captivity captive and giving gifts to men (Ephesians 4:8; Psalm 68:18). He triumphed over principalities and powers, making an open show of them (Colossians 2:15) and now leads the march that advances the gospel into the earth—'thanks be to God, who always leads us in triumphal procession in Christ, and manifests through us the sweet aroma of the knowledge of him in every place' (2 Corinthians 2:14).

(5) Celebration

Fifthly, marching for Jesus involves celebration. Old Testament religious festivals included feasting and celebration as well as worship and prayer. They used to eat well and enjoy themselves—holy days included celebration. To reflect this spirit of celebration our marches have a carnival feel to them. Some folk put on clowns' suits, others wear bright clothing, we carry balloons and colourful banners, there's lively music and songs—all in celebration of God's extravagant love for the world.

If you work in the inner city you know you've got to celebrate. If you go to the poor and disadvantaged and take the drab religion and dull meetings that some of us suffer, you won't get much of a hearing. Worse, you are doing a lot of damage. They have enough problems already without the problems of morbid religiosity. If you work in the inner city you must go and assert life because people who live there are dying. You have to assert wholeness because there's sadness and depression. You have to assert life in relationships because so often families are falling apart. As we go in with celebration we are communicating the character and heart of God so that people know that this is what Christianity is really about.

In Nehemiah's day Ezra and his colleagues read the Scriptures to the people and instructed them. As they gathered and worshipped, the crowd began to weep, confessing their sin (Nehemiah 8:9). However, Ezra and Nehemiah went around saying, 'Stop crying! Be quiet! Enjoy yourselves! Here's a bottle of wine for you and some meat for you. Take it to those who haven't even come, that they might be blessed also!'

So they asserted victory and celebration into the context

of defeat and disillusionment. We seek to do the same in our cities as we march for God.

(6) Prophetic symbolism

Sixthly, marching for Jesus involves prophetic symbolism. Moses lifted up his rod and the Red Sea opened (Exodus 14:16), God 'king-ed it', he actively exerted his royal power into the earth on the back of the prophet's word. (Exodus 15:18 is the first time in the Bible that God is said to reign.) What Moses actually said was 'Stand still,' but the prophetic 'word' that released God's power was a symbolic act—the lifting of his hand holding the rod.

Joshua led the people of Israel in marching around the walls of Jericho as a prophetic act (Joshua 6). On the completion of the seventh circuit on the seventh day the walls came down. There was no cause/effect relationship between their marching and the walls collapsing. There was no cause/effect relationship between Moses lifting the rod and the sea opening. The dividing of the sea and the collapse of the walls was God directly intervening, 'kinging it' on the back of the prophetic word. When we march we are making a prophetic statement; it is prophetic symbolism.

Jehoshaphat marched into the desert with the choir in front of him. As they stood singing and praising God confusion arose among their enemies who then proceeded to destroy each other (2 Chronicles 20:21ff)! That too was a prophetic act. Nehemiah organised a march around the walls of Jerusalem also as prophetic symbolism, incidentally with a purpose exactly opposite to Joshua's—to firm the walls up (Nehemiah 12:31,38)! Jesus comes on the first Resurrection day and breathes on his disciples—'Receive the Holy Spirit' (John 20:22) and fifty days later it is fulfilled at Pentecost. When we march we are acting prophetically to release the Holy Spirit—to 'let out' the God who inhabits our praises. He moves out from us into the streets so he can run through people's lives, into the dark and dirty places, the gutters of life, to bring holiness back into society.

When Agabus put Paul's hands in his belt and tied them up it was again prophetic symbolism, not so much to bring it about, but to demonstrate what lay in store for Paul, to give a picture so that people could understand. In the same way marching for Jesus gives spiritual understanding to people.

(7) Claiming the ground

Seventhly, as we march for Jesus, there is a sense in which we are claiming the ground on which we walk. When the Spirit of God came on Azuza Street in 1906, they said you could feel the love of God for a quarter of a mile around the building. This was simply because God the Holy Spirit acts territorially just as evil spirits do. Theoretical Christians find this hard to grasp. They assert that God is everywhere and the Holy Spirit is omnipresent—which of course is true, but is only part of the truth.

At Azuza Street the Holy Spirit who is everywhere intensified and focused his presence in a certain building. Similarly the God who is everywhere became 'somewhere' at Bethlehem when Christ was born. At Pentecost, the Spirit who is everywhere became somewhere. He didn't come to Galilee, or Nazareth, or Capernaum. The Spirit of God came to Jerusalem, to a specific place in Jerusalem—and there was a territorial awareness that God was in that place because he had come upon the temple of his people.

It is not therefore surprising that the Holy Spirit sometimes affects the actual building where people are gathered—'after they had prayed the place where they were meeting was shaken' (Acts 4:31). Again in Isaiah 6:4 'at the sound of their [angelic] voices the doorposts and thresholds [of the temple] shook'.

In a similar way the church on the march gives an opportunity for God to be manifest on the streets in a certain place at a certain time. We are saying, 'Everywhere the sole of my foot treads I am taking for the Lord' (see Joshua 1:3). Why should the enemy have this territory? Why should he

rule in our streets and control our economics? Why should
education be dominated by atheists and humanists? We put
our feet down on a bit of territory and we say, 'Lord, this
is your ground and the meek shall inherit the earth'
(Matthew 5:5). We don't do it with violence and guns,
we don't do it with aggressive shouts, we do it with
happiness, with joy, and by putting our feet down and saying
'The meek shall inherit the earth' because Jesus has
promised it.

When Christians all over the earth put their feet down
and join hands declaring: 'This bit of territory is the Lord's,
the earth is the Lord's and the fullness thereof (Psalm 24:1),
your kingdom come, your will be done on earth as it is in
heaven' (Matthew 6:10), then there will be a great net of
the kingdom ready for Jesus to pull in (Matthew 13:47). He
will separate out the bad (because there is bad in the
kingdom as well as good) and having made that division he
will set up a kingdom where everything is good. Not just a
net, but a blanket of goodness as the kingdoms of this world
become the kingdom of our God and his Christ (Revelation
11:15).

Two thousand years before Calvary Abraham, the first
prophet of the Bible (Genesis 20:7) and the root of the
prophetic church today, prophesied to Isaac on the way up
the mountain, 'My son, God will provide himself a lamb'
(Genesis 22:8). That was the only bit of verbal prophesying
he ever did. It was magnificent and pointed to the Lamb of
God that would take away the sin of the world. But there
was more to it than that. When he got to the top he didn't
say much but he continued to act prophetically. He put his
son on the altar, took a knife, tried to bring it down and
asked God to help him. The sun glinted on the blade and
it flashed in his eyes. He saw what he thought would be the
last heave of his son's breast but heard the words, 'Abraham,
Abraham, do not stretch out your hand against the lad, and
do nothing to him; for now I know that you fear God, since
you have not withheld your son, your only son, from me'
(Genesis 22:12). In that moment Abraham had a glimpse

of the future still two thousand years away. (Jesus said, 'Abraham saw my day and rejoiced', John 8:56.)

Abraham was a prophet, a 'seer' and he 'saw' the day two thousand years later when Jesus would be crucified in that very area of Moriah. God would do exactly what Abraham had already symbolically acted out. I believe Abraham was claiming that ground for God's activity. I believe he was saying, 'This bit of ground is for God, I've taken it for him.' It might be argued, 'What if he hadn't made that journey, offered his son and said those words?' Well, possibly God would have found somebody else and maybe another place, and then the whole story of God's unfolding plan would have been different. But as it was, he found a faithful man who claimed the ground and took it by a symbolic act. This is recorded for our instruction and encouragement. I believe that we are meant to claim the whole earth in a similar way. The mission of the church all over the world is to speak and act prophetically so that God's will gets done on earth, as it is in heaven (Matthew 6:10; Romans 4:13).

The march of God through history

We have looked at seven reasons why we should march for Jesus. Let me make one last point.

Jesus marched physically out of the grave in a resurrection body and went to heaven. We don't say he did it all spiritually, cerebrally, conceptually; he did it literally. He went physically into the grave and marched physically up into heaven. I believe this helps us to understand not only that we do march in a spiritual sense through our spiritual pilgrimage, but there are times when God asks us to march physically as well. In doing so we are following in the steps of others in history.

God didn't always ask the Israelites to march when they moved from place to place, but when they left Egypt, he instructed them to march in battle formation (the Hebrew of Exodus 13:18 says that they lined up in ranks of five as they marched with the ark in their midst). This is one of the first great marches of the Bible. As they moved out in military style from Egypt they began to discover what it felt like to be free. 'We are away from the whip of the taskmaster, we are getting out of Egypt, we are going to live and share together voluntarily instead of by compulsion as slaves. Hallelujah!' Marching is equally good for us today.

Interpreting the Old Testament in the light of the New, we say that Jesus died and carried us through the Red Sea of death. We've been baptised into Christ as they were baptised into Moses. We have come up on resurrection ground.

Many Christians need a little bit of physical marching to help them to get loose spiritually. It frees us up! It is a poor army that never marches! We get out in the open, marching along, and we start to become liberated in our spirits. I'm sure you've experienced this: you're in your room trying to pray and you feel a spiritual heaviness, so you think, 'I'll go out and walk and pray in the open air.'

As we claim the territory of our inheritance in Christ we meet great resistance, just as the advance of the people of Israel under Joshua was opposed by citadels. These strongholds need to be brought down, and marching for Jesus is a way of removing the resistance in the spiritual atmosphere. David and a group of worshippers carried the ark back into Jerusalem and the psalm celebrating the occasion includes the words, 'Ascribe honour and glory to him all you nations. Ascribe to the Lord all the peoples of the earth, power and glory' (1 Chronicles 16:28). In a similar way our worship on the streets carries God's presence into society. Like David in his psalm, we also declare to the peoples of the earth that they should worship the Lord and ascribe honour to Jesus. And that is exactly what often happens; somebody gets converted during a march because by worship we proclaim, and by proclaiming we worship. As we mix worship, prayer and prophecy together the Lord is exalted and the kingdom advances.

When Jehoshaphat got the people praying and praising it

brought confusion to their enemies. In a similar way a worshipping people who get out and penetrate the spiritual atmosphere confuse the enemy and weaken his grip upon society. Victory on the scale of Jehoshaphat's is then also possible for us today. As previously mentioned, Nehemiah found that praise and prayer provided a way of strengthening the walls he had built around Jerusalem. He marched around them reinforcing what was good. Joshua demolished walls, Nehemiah built them up. Even today in our society there are often prayers when buildings are opened, at the beginning of each day's business in Parliament, and at the launching of a ship. Why? Because there is a sense that with a public act you are actually shoring up and strengthening what requires protection and reinforcement. We believe that's what our society requires today. The good must be affirmed and strengthened by our prayers.

In the final six months of his ministry Jesus did a freedom march from Caeserea Philippi southwards all the way down the Jordan valley and up through Jericho with a mass of people gathered behind him. This freedom march culminated in the procession into Jerusalem with Jesus riding on an ass. There he was to confront Caiaphas, Pilate and Herod who between them headed up the three main forces of the day entrenched within Jerusalem. As Jesus rode in physically, an impact was made into the spiritual realm.

The opposite kingdom was coming. When Jesus went to the cross he was not wrestling against flesh and blood. With his hands outstretched he gripped the spiritual powers and grappled with them, holding them down in the same way as a person's head is forced under water until he drowns. Jesus held Satan there and then announced with a great shout of triumph, 'It is finished!' He then leapt into the grave and rose victorious over death and Satan, hell and sin. By that mighty march culminating in the cross he defeated the powers of darkness. He marched through the cross leading captivity captive with every spiritual power under his feet (Colossians 2:14,15). Rising up to heaven, he marched past Satan, past the authorities, principalities

and powers, past thrones and dominions, and as he passed
they all had to bow the knee and say, 'Jesus is Lord of all.'
Even Satan has to bow and confess that Jesus Christ is Lord
(Ephesians 4:10; Hebrews 4:14). Satan hates it but he has
to do it because the march goes right on into the heart of
God. In the heart of heaven every power that exists is now
under the feet of Jesus, because Jesus Christ is Lord of all.
This is what we are declaring, proclaiming and symbolising.
This is what we are letting loose when we march for Jesus.
It's wonderful theology expressed in simple obedience and
faith as we march.

I'm looking forward to the final great march when Jesus
comes back again, when the heavens open up and the saints
follow after him, clothed in white robes and riding on white
horses. Instead of that weak body of ours, that 'old ass'
which, in St Francis' words, which needs kicking along now
and then, we will have a glorious body like his – a 'white
horse'? (Revelation 19:11–16) At the front of the march
Jesus will ride on a white horse at the head of a new
humanity. It will not only be a march, it will be a ride and
we will ride after him, right across the heavens. Armies of
angels will follow us. Principalities and powers will bow.
The angels will begin to give way and give place to the saints
because the age to come is not put under the power of angels,
it is put under the feet of the saints (Hebrews 2:5) – we will
judge the world and the angels (1 Corinthians 6:2,3).

We will ride with the King into all the wonder of eternity,
following the Lamb wherever he goes (Revelation 14:4),
marching on to the farthest galaxies of the universe and into
all sorts of other dimensional worlds that we have never
even dreamed exist. There we will know that the greatest
thing of all is that we have marched with Jesus, are still
marching with the King, and now see him face to face
(Revelation 22:7).

For further information about March for Jesus in the United
Kingdom contact:

March for Jesus
PO Box 39
Sunbury-on-Thames
Middlesex
TW16 6PP
Telephone: 0932 789681
Fax: 0903 789691

Prayerwalking

by Graham Kendrick & John Houghton

Are you praying effectively for the place where you live? The people, the clubs, pubs and shops; the schools and the leisure centres?

Prayerwalking will get you and your church out on the streets, and bring the power of prayer to the enemy's gates.

'Visionary, inspiring, powerful - simple and practical, so easy to fit into our everyday lifestyle.'

CHRIS LEAGUE, UK Co-ordinator, Lydia Fellowship

'Jesus said to watch and pray - this book takes that command literally. I highly recommend it.'

FLOYD McCLUNG, Executive International Director,
Youth With A Mission

'We must soak our land in prayer. *Prayerwalking* will help us do just that.'
GERALD COATES, Leader of Pioneer Team
and joint organiser of March for Jesus

'*Prayerwalking* - as old as the Bible, vital for spiritual warfare, a catalyst for an advancing church.'

ROGER FORSTER, Leader of Ichthus Fellowship, London

'Perspiring and practical prayer! A must for anyone interested in revival.'
SANDY MILLAR, Vicar of Holy Trinity Church,
Brompton Road, London

(A5 handbook)

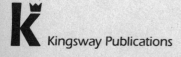

Kingsway Publications

Make Way, Public Praise

by Graham Kendrick

During recent years, hundreds of thousands of people have taken up Graham Kendrick's call to take their praise onto the streets.

This march handbook comprises 45 songs suitable for street praise from *Shine, Jesus, Shine, A Carnival of Praise, The Gift* and *The Cross*. Starting with *Shine, Jesus, Shine*, this book takes the user through Graham's first four marches, arranged in individual sections, and includes comprehensive notes and suggestions to assist groups and churches to organise and make the best out of their public expression of praise.

The words-only sections have been designed to be reproduced by Church Copyright Licence holders for use in marches.